JAMES BALDWIN

The Amen Corner

James Baldwin was born in 1924 and educated in New York. He is the author of more than twenty works of fiction and nonfiction, including *Go Tell It on the Mountain; Notes of a Native Son; Giovanni's Room; Nobody Knows My Name; Another Country; The Fire Next Time; Nothing Personal; Blues for Mister Charlie; Going to Meet the Man; The Amen Corner; Tell Me How Long the Train's Been Gone; One Day When I Was Lost; No Name in the Street; If Beale Street Could Talk; The Devil Finds Work; Little Man, Little Man; Just Above My Head; The Evidence of Things Not Seen; Jimmy's Blues;* and *The Price of the Ticket.* Among the awards he received are a Eugene F. Saxon Memorial Trust Award, a Rosenwald Fellowship, a Guggenheim Fellowship, a *Partisan Review* Fellowship, and a Ford Foundation grant. He was made a Commander of the Legion of Honor in 1986. He died in 1987.

INTERNATIONAL

ALSO BY JAMES BALDWIN

THE AMEN CORNER

THE AMEN CORNER

A Play by

JAMES BALDWIN

VINTAGE INTERNATIONAL
Vintage Books
A Division of Random House, Inc.
New York

FIRST VINTAGE INTERNATIONAL EDITION, FEBRUARY 1998

Copyright © 1968 by James Baldwin
Copyright renewed 1996 by The James Baldwin Estate

All rights reserved under International and Pan-American
Copyright Conventions. Published in the United States
by Vintage Books, a division of Random House, Inc., New York,
and simultaneously in Canada by Random House of Canada
Limited, Toronto. Originally published in hardcover in the
United States by The Dial Press, New York, in 1968.

Baldwin, James, 1924–
The amen corner : a play / by James Baldwin.
p. cm.
ISBN 0-375-70188-5
1. Afro-American churches—New York (State)—
New York—Drama. 2. Afro-American families—
New York (State)—New York—Drama.
3. Harlem (New York, N.Y.)—Drama. I. Title.
PS3552.A45A8   1998
812'.54—DC21   97-35624
CIP

Random House Web address: www.randomhouse.com

Printed in the United States of America
10

Caution: Professionals and amateurs are hereby warned that
The Amen Corner, being fully protected by copyright, is subject to royalties.
All rights including professional, amateur, motion picture, recitation,
lecturing, public reading, radio and television broadcasting, and rights
of translation into foreign language are strictly reserved.

For
Nina, Ray, Miles, Bird,
and
Billie

The Amen Corner

THE AMEN CORNER

WRITING *The Amen Corner* I remember as a desperate and even rather irresponsible act—it was certainly considered irresponsible by my agent at that time. She did not wish to discourage me, but it was her duty to let me know that the American theatre was not exactly clamoring for plays on obscure aspects of Negro life, especially one written by a virtually unknown author whose principal effort until that time had been one novel. She may sincerely have believed that I had gotten my signals mixed and earnestly explained to me that, with one novel under my belt, it was the *magazine* world that was open to me, *not* the world of the theatre; I sensibly ought to be pursuing the avenue that was open, especially since I had no money at all. I couldn't explain to her or to myself why I wasted so much time on a play. I knew, for one thing, that very few novelists are able to write plays and I really had no reason to suppose that I could be an exception to this age-old, iron rule. I was perfectly aware that it would probably never be produced, and, furthermore, I didn't even have any ambition to conquer the theatre. To this last point we shall return, for I was being very dishonest, or perhaps merely very cunning, with myself concerning the extent of my ambition.

I had written one novel, *Go Tell It on the Mountain,* and it had taken me a long time, nearly ten years, to do it. Those ten years had taken me from Harlem, through the horrors of being a civilian employee (unskilled) of the Army in New Jersey, to being an unskilled employee, period. There is no point in trying to describe the sheer physical terror which was my life in those days, for I was simply grotesquely out of my setting and everyone around me knew it, and made me pay for it. I say "everyone" for the sake of convenience, for there were, indeed, exceptions, thank God, and these exceptions helped to save my life and also taught me what I then most bitterly needed to know—*i.e.*, that love and compassion, which always arrive in such unexpected packages, have nothing to do with the color of anybody's skin. For I was simply another black boy; there were millions like me at the mercy of the labor market, to say nothing of the labor unions, and it was very clear to me that in the jungle in which I found myself I had no future at all: my going under was simply a matter of time.

But, on the other hand, I had a family—a mother and eight younger brothers and sisters—and something in me knew that if I were to betray them and the love we bore each other, I would be destroying myself. Yet there was no possibility that I would ever be of any use to them, or anyone else, if I continued my life in factories. I was, unfortunately, not equipped for anything but hard labor. No one would ever look at me and offer me anything more than a menial job, and yet people very frequently hesitated to offer me the only jobs open to me because they obscurely felt that I was unreliable, probably inflammatory, and far more trouble than I could possibly be worth. Well, to tell the truth, I can't say very much about those years; I suppose I've blotted it out. What I did, finally, was allow myself to drop to the very bottom of the labor market, became a busboy and short-order cook in places like Riker's—and wrote all the time. And when I was twenty-four, I took the last of a Rosenwald Fellowship grant and bought a plane ticket to Paris. I bought a plane ticket because I was afraid I would lose my nerve if I waited for a boat. I got to Paris with forty dollars and no French. I slid downhill with impressive speed, which wasn't difficult considering the slightness of my eminence, ended up, successively, in one French hospital and one French jail, and then took stock. I was twenty-five and didn't have much to show for it. I started again. By 1952, I finished *Mountain,* borrowed money from Marlon Brando, one of the great and beautiful exceptions referred to above, and came home to try to sell it. I came home in the summertime, and it may have been the emotional climate and the events of that summer which caused me to write *The Amen Corner.*

I had been away for four years—four very crucial and definitive years. I myself have described my exile as a self-exile, but it was really far more complex and bitter than that. No one really wishes to leave his homeland. I left because I was driven out, because my homeland would not allow me to grow in the only direction in which I could grow. This is but another way of saying that all my country-men had been able to offer me during the twenty-four years that I tried to live here was death—and death, moreover, on their terms. I had been lucky enough to defeat their intention, and, physically, I had escaped. But I had not escaped myself, I had not escaped my antecedents, not even France could compensate for some of the things I knew and felt that I was losing; no Frenchman or French-woman could meet me with the speed and fire of some black boys and girls whom I remembered and whom I missed; they did not know enough about me to be able to correct me. It is true that they met me with something else—themselves, in fact—and taught me things I did not know (how to take a deep breath, for example) and corrected me in unexpected and rather painful ways. But it was not really my home. I might live there forever and it would never be my home. No matter how immensely I might become reconciled to my condition, it was, nevertheless, the specialness of my condi-tion which had driven me to France. And I had to know this; I could not, on pain of death, forget it—or, rather, to forget it would mean that my high pretensions were nothing but a fraud, that the anguish of my forebears meant nothing to me, and that I had never really intended to become a writer but had only been trying to be safe.

In New York that summer all this became very vivid to me—as vivid as a wound; and it was I, it seemed to me, who had become a kind of ambulating anguish. Not only had New York not changed —as far as I could see, it had become worse; and my hope of ever being able to live in New York diminished with every hour. And this distress was inconceivably aggravated by the one circumstance which would have seemed to be able to alleviate it: the fact that I was a young writer, with a small reputation and a possible future, whose first novel was about to be published. But, to tell the truth, I was really a young *Negro* writer, and the world into which I was moving quite helplessly, and quite without malice, had its own expectations of me, expectations which I was determined to defeat.

The editor assigned to me and my book asked me, when I entered his office for the first time and after the book had been accepted, "What about all that come-to-Jesus stuff? Don't you think you ought to take it out?" *Go Tell It on the Mountain* is the study of a Negro evangelist and his family. They do, indeed, talk in a "come-to-Jesus" idiom, but to "take it out" could only mean that my editor was suggesting that I burn the book. I gagged, literally, and began to sweat, ran to the water cooler, tried to pull myself together, and returned to the office to explain the intention of my novel. I learned a great deal that afternoon; learned, to put it far too briefly, what I was up against; took the check and went back to Paris.

I went back to Paris, as I then thought, for good, and my reasons this time seemed very different from the reasons which had driven me there in the first place. My original reasons were that I had been forced, most reluctantly, to recognize that thought was also action; what one saw, the point of view from which one viewed the world, dictated what one did; and this meant, in my situation, that I was in danger, most literally, of *thinking* myself out of existence. I was not expected to know the things I knew, or to say the things I said, to make the kind of jokes I made, or to do the things I did. I knew that I was a black street-boy, and that knowledge was all I had. I could not delude myself about it. I did not even have the rather deadly temptations of being good-looking, for I knew that I was not good-looking. All I had, in a word, was me, and I was forced to insist on this *me* with all the energy I had. Naturally, I got my head broken, naturally people laughed when I said I was going to be a writer, and naturally, since I wanted to live, I finally split the scene. But when I came back to sell my first novel, I realized that I was being corraled into another trap: now I was a writer, a *Negro* writer, and I was expected to write diminishing versions of *Go Tell It on the Mountain* forever.

Which I refused to do. I had not, after all, paid all those dues for that. I had no idea whether or not I could write a play, but I was absolutely determined that I would not, not at that moment in my career, not at that moment in my life, attempt another novel. I did not trust myself to do it. I was really terrified that I would, without even knowing that I was doing it, try to repeat my first success and begin to imitate myself. I knew that I had more to say and much, much more to discover than I had been able to indicate in *Mountain*. Poverty is not a crime in Paris; it does not mean that you are a worthless person; and so I returned and began what I told myself was a "writing exercise": by which I meant I'm still a young man, my family now knows that I really am a writer—that was very important to me—let us now see if I am equipped to go the distance, and let's try something we've never tried before. The first line written in *The Amen Corner* is now Margaret's line in the Third Act: "It's a awful thing to think about, the way love never dies!" That line, of course, says a great deal about me—the play says a great deal about me—but I was thinking not only, not merely, about the terrifying desolation of my private life but about the great burdens carried by my father. I was old enough by now, at last, to recognize the nature of the dues he had paid, old enough to wonder if I could possibly have paid them, old enough, at last, at last, to know that I had loved him and had wanted him to love me. I could see that the nature of the battle we had fought had been dictated by the fact that our temperaments were so fatally the same: neither of us could bend. And when I began to think about what had happened to him, I began to see why he was so terrified of what was surely going to happen to me.

The Amen Corner comes somewhere out of that. For to think about my father meant that I had also to think about my mother and the stratagems she was forced to use to save her children from the destruction awaiting them just outside her door. It is because I know what Sister Margaret goes through, and what her male child is menaced by, that I become so unmanageable when people ask me to confirm their hope that there has been *progress*—what a word! —in white-black relations. There has certainly not been enough progress to solve Sister Margaret's dilemma: how to treat her husband and her son as men and at the same time to protect them from the bloody consequences of trying to be a man in this society. No one yet knows, or is in the least prepared to speculate on, how high a bill we will yet have to pay for what we have done to Negro men and women. She is in the church because her society has left her no other place to go. Her sense of reality is dictated by the society's assumption, which also becomes her own, of her inferiority. Her need for human affirmation, and also for vengeance, expresses itself in her merciless piety; and her love, which is real but which is also at the mercy of her genuine and absolutely justifiable terror, turns her into a tyrannical matriarch. In all of this, of course, she loses her old self—the fiery, fast-talking little black woman whom Luke loved. Her triumph, which is also, if I may say so, the historical triumph of the Negro people in this country, is that she sees this finally and accepts it, and, although she has lost everything, also gains the keys to the kingdom. The kingdom is love, and love is selfless, although only the self can lead one there. She gains herself.

One last thing: concerning my theatrical ambitions, and my cunning or dishonesty—I was armed, I knew, in attempting to write the play, by the fact that I was born in the church. I knew that out of the ritual of the church, historically speaking, comes the act of the theatre, the *communion* which is the theatre. And I knew that what I wanted to do in the theatre was to recreate moments I remembered as a boy preacher, to involve the people, even against their will, to shake them up, and, hopefully, to change them. I knew that an unknown black writer could not possibly hope to achieve this forum.

I did not want to enter the theatre on the theatre's terms, but on mine. And so I waited. And the fact that *The Amen Corner* took ten years to reach the professional stage says a great deal more about the American theatre than it says about this author. The American Negro really is a part of this country, and on the day we face this fact, and not before that day, we will become a nation and possibly a great one.

James Baldwin

ACT I

A SUNDAY MORNING IN HARLEM

ACT II

THE FOLLOWING SATURDAY AFTERNOON

ACT III

THE NEXT MORNING

All the action takes place on
a unit set which is the church and home
of Margaret Alexander.

CAST OF CHARACTERS

MARGARET ALEXANDER	Pastor of the church
ODESSA	Margaret's older sister
IDA JACKSON	A young woman
SISTER MOORE	
SISTER BOXER	} Elders of the church
BROTHER BOXER	
DAVID	Margaret's eighteen-year-old son
LUKE	Her husband
SISTER SALLY	
SISTER DOUGLASS	
SISTER RICE	} Members of the congregation
BROTHER DAVIS	
BROTHER WASHINGTON	
WOMAN	
OTHER MEMBERS OF THE CONGREGATION	

ACT I

We are facing the scrim wall of the tenement which holds the home and church of SISTER MARGARET ALEXANDER.

It is a very bright Sunday morning.

Before the curtain rises, we hear street sounds, laughter, cursing, snatches of someone's radio; and under everything, the piano, which DAVID is playing in the church.

When the scrim rises we see, stage right, the church, which is dominated by the pulpit, on a platform, upstage. On the platform, a thronelike chair. On the pulpit, an immense open Bible.

To the right of the pulpit, the piano, the top of which is cluttered with hymnbooks and tambourines.

Just below the pulpit, a table, flanked by two plain chairs. On the table two collection plates, one brass, one straw, two Bibles, perhaps a vase of artificial flowers. Facing the pulpit, and running the length of the church, the camp chairs for the congregation.

To the right, downstage, the door leading to the street.

The church is on a level above the apartment and should give the impression of dominating the family's living quarters.

The apartment is stage left. Upstage, the door leading to the church; perhaps a glimpse of the staircase. Downstage, the kitchen, cluttered: a new Frigidaire, prominently placed, kitchen table with dishes on it, suitcase open on a chair.

Downstage, left, LUKE's bedroom. A small, dark room with a bed, a couple of chairs, a hassock, odds and ends thrown about in it as though it has long been used as a storage room. The room ends in a small door which leads to the rest of the house.

Members of the congregation almost always enter the church by way of the street door, stage right. Members of

5

the family almost always enter the church by way of the inside staircase. The apartment door is stage left of the kitchen.

At rise, there is a kind of subdued roar and humming, out of which is heard the music prologue, "The Blues Is Man," which segues into a steady rollicking beat, and we see the congregation singing.

ALL:

One day I walked the lonesome road
The spirit spoke unto me
And filled my heart with love—
Yes, he filled my heart with love,
Yes, he filled my heart with love,
And he wrote my name above,
And that's why I thank God I'm in His care.

(CHORUS)

Let me tell you now
Whilst I'm in His care,
I'm in my Saviour's care,
Jesus got His arms wrapped around me,
No evil thoughts can harm me
'Cause I'm so glad I'm in His care.

CONTRALTO:

I opened my Bible and began to read
About all the things He's done for me;
Read on down about Chapter One
How He made the earth then He made the sun.
Read on down about Chapter Two
How He died for me and He died for you.

6

Read on down about Chapter Three
How He made the blind, the blind to see.
Read on down about Chapter Four
How He healed the sick and blessed the poor.
Read on down about Chapter Five
How it rained forty days and Noah survived.
Six, seven, about the same
Just keep praising my Jesus' name.
Read on down about Chapter Eight,
The golden streets and the pearly gates.
Read on down about Chapter Nine
We all get to heaven in due time.
Read on down about Chapter Ten
My God's got the key and He'll let me in.
When I finish reading the rest
I'll go to judgment to stand my test.
He'll say come a little higher, come a little higher,
He'll say come a little higher and take your seat.

ALL:

Let me tell you now
Whilst I'm in His care,
I'm in my Saviour's care,
Jesus got His arms wrapped around me,
No evil thoughts can harm me
'Cause I'm so glad I'm in His care.

MARGARET: Amen! Let the church say amen!
ALL: Amen! Hallelujah! Amen!
MARGARET: And let us say amen again!

ALL: Amen! Amen!

MARGARET: Because the Lord God Almighty—the King of *Kings*, amen!—had sent out the word, "Set thine house in order, for thou shalt die and not live." And King Hezekiah turned his face to the wall.

ODESSA: Amen!

SISTER MOORE: Preach it, daughter! Preach it this morning!

MARGARET: Now, when the king got the message, amen, he didn't do like some of us do today. He didn't go running to no spiritualists, no, he didn't. He didn't spend a lot of money on no fancy doctors, he didn't break his neck trying to commit himself to Bellevue Hospital. He sent for the prophet, Isaiah. Amen. He sent for a saint of God.

SISTER BOXER: Well, amen!

MARGARET: Now, children, you know this king had a mighty kingdom. There were many souls in that kingdom. He had rich and poor, high and low, amen! And I believe he had a lot of preachers around, puffed up and riding around in chariots —just like they is today, bless God—and stealing from the poor.

ALL: Amen!

MARGARET: But the king didn't call on none of them. No. He called on Isaiah. He called on Isaiah, children, because Isaiah lived a holy life. He wasn't one of them always running in and out of the king's palace. When the king gave a party, I doubt that he even thought of inviting him. You know how people do, amen: Well, let's not have him. Let's not have her. They too sanctified. They too holy. Amen! They don't drink, they don't smoke, they don't go to the movies, they don't curse, they don't play cards, they don't covet their neighbor's husband or their neighbor's wife—well, amen! They just holy. If we invite that sanctified fool they just going to make everybody else feel uncomfortable!

ALL: Well, bless the Lord! Amen!

MARGARET: But let the trouble come. Oh, let the trouble come. They don't go to none of them they sees all the time, amen. No, they don't go running to the people they was playing cards with all night long. When the trouble comes, look like they just can't stand none of their former ways—and they go a-digging back in their minds, in their memories, looking for a saint of God. Oh, yes! I've seen it happen time and time again and I know some of you out there this morning, you've seen it happen too. Sometimes, bless the Lord, you be in the woman's kitchen, washing up her cocktail glasses, amen, and maybe singing praises to the Lord. And pretty soon, here she come, this woman who maybe ain't said two words to you all the time you been working there. She draw up a chair and she say, "Can I talk to you, sister?" She got a houseful of people but she ain't gone to them. She in the kitchen, amen, talking to a saint of God. Because the world is watching you, children, even when you think the whole world's asleep!

ALL: Amen! Amen!

MARGARET: But, dearly beloved, she can't come to you—the world can't come to you—if you don't live holy. This way of holiness is a hard way. I know some of you think Sister Margaret's too hard on you. She don't want you to do this and she won't let you do that. Some of you say, "Ain't no harm in reading the funny papers." But children, *yes*, there's harm in it. While you reading them funny papers, your mind ain't on the Lord. And if your mind ain't stayed on Him, every hour of the day, Satan's going to cause you to fall. Amen! Some of you say, "Ain't no harm in me working for a liquor company. I ain't going to be drinking the liquor, I'm just going to be driving the *truck!*" But a saint of God ain't got no business delivering liquor to folks all day—how

9

you going to spend all day helping folks into hell and then think you going to come here in the evening and help folks into heaven? It can't be done. The Word tells me, No man can serve two masters!

ALL: Well, the Word *do* say it! Bless the Lord!

MARGARET: Let us think about the Word this morning, children. Let it take root in your hearts: "Set thine house in order, for thou shalt die and not live."

(MARGARET *begins to sing and instantly* DAVID *strikes up another "shout" song and the congregation sings—loud, violent, clapping of hands, tambourines, etc.* MARGARET *rises and sits.*)

MARGARET:

I got the holy spirit

To help me run this race.

I got the holy spirit,

It appointed my soul a place.

My faith looks up to heaven,

I know up there I'll see

The Father, the Son, the Holy Spirit

Watching over me.

BARITONE:

Once I was a sinner

Treading a sinful path;

Never thought about Jesus

Or the fate of His wrath.

Then I met the Saviour

And ever since that day

I been walking my faith,

Praying with love,

Looking up above.
With His arms around me,
I'm just leaning on Him.
For there is no other
On Him I can depend.
When my life is ended
And I lay these burdens down
I'm gonna walk with faith,
Pray with love,
Looking from above.

ALL:

I got the holy spirit
To help me run this race.
I got the holy spirit,
It appointed my soul a place.
My faith looks up to heaven,
I know up there I'll see
The Father, the Son, the Holy Spirit
Watching over me.
(SISTER MOORE *comes forward. The excitement begins to subside.*)

SISTER MOORE: Well, I know our souls is praising God this morning!

ALL: Amen!

SISTER MOORE: It ain't every flock blessed to have a shepherd like Sister Margaret. Let's praise God for her!

ALL: Amen! Amen!

SISTER MOORE: Now, I ain't here to take up a lot of your time, amen. Sister Margaret's got to go off from us this afternoon to visit our sister church in Philadelphia. There's many sick up there, amen! Old Mother Phillips is sick in the body and some of her congregation is sick in the soul. And our pastor done give her word that she'd go up there and try to strengthen the feeble knees. Bless God!

(*Music begins and underlines her speech.*)

Before we close out this order of service, I'd like to say, I praise the Lord for being here, I thank Him for my life, health and strength. I want to thank Him for the way He's worked with me these many long years and I want to thank Him for keeping me *humble!* I want to thank Him for keeping me pure and set apart from the lusts of the flesh, for protecting me—hallelujah!—from all carnal temptation. When I come before my Maker, I'm going to come before Him *pure.* I'm going to say "Bless your name, Jesus, no man has ever touched me!" Hallelujah!

(*Congregation begins to sing.*)

ALL:

Come to Jesus, come to Jesus,

Come to Jesus, just now.

Come to Jesus, come to Jesus just now.

He will save you, He will save you,

He will save you, just now.

He will save you, He will save you just now.

SISTER MOORE: Now before we raise the sacrifice offering, the Lord has led *me,* amen, to ask if there's a soul in this congregation who wants to ask the Lord's especial attention to them this morning? Any sinners, amen, any backsliders? Don't you be ashamed, you just come right on up here to the altar.

(*Tentative music on the piano.*)

Don't hold back, dear ones. Is there any sick in the building? The Lord's hand is outstretched.

(*Silence.*)

Come, dear hearts, don't hold back.

(*Toward the back of the church, a young woman, not dressed in white, rises. She holds a baby in her arms.*)

Yes, honey, come on up here. Don't be ashamed.

(*The congregation turns to look at the young woman. She hesitates.* MARGARET *rises and steps forward.*)

MARGARET: Come on, daughter!

(*The young woman comes up the aisle. Approving murmurs come from the congregation.* SISTER MOORE *steps a little aside.*)

That's right, daughter. The Word say, If you make one step, He'll make two. Just step out on the promise. What's your name, daughter?

YOUNG WOMAN: Jackson. Mrs. Ida Jackson.

SISTER MOORE (*to the congregation*): Sister Ida Jackson. Bless the Lord!

ALL: Bless her!

MARGARET: And what's the name of that little one?

MRS. JACKSON: His name is Daniel. He been sick. I want you to pray for him.

(*She begins to weep.*)

MARGARET: Dear heart, don't you weep this morning. I know what that emptiness feel like. What's been ailing this baby?

MRS. JACKSON: I don't know. Done took him to the doctor and the doctor, he don't know. He can't keep nothing on his little stomach and he cry all night, every night, and he done got real puny. Sister, I done lost one child already, please pray the Lord to make this baby well!

MARGARET (*steps down and touches* MRS. JACKSON): Don't fret, little sister. Don't you fret this morning. The Lord is mighty to save. This here's a Holy Ghost station. (*To the congregation*) Ain't that so, dear ones?

ALL: Amen!

MARGARET: He a right fine little boy. Why ain't your husband here with you this morning?

MRS. JACKSON: I guess he at the house. He done got so evil and bitter, looks like he don't never want to hear me mention the Lord's name. He don't know I'm here this morning.
(Sympathetic murmurs from the congregation. MARGARET *watches* MRS. JACKSON.)

MARGARET: You poor little thing. You ain't much more than a baby yourself, is you? Sister, is you ever confessed the Lord as your personal Saviour? Is you trying to lead a life that's pleasing to Him?

MRS. JACKSON: Yes, ma'am. I'm trying every day.

MARGARET: Is your husband trying as hard as you?

MRS. JACKSON: I ain't got no fault to find with him.

MARGARET: Maybe the Lord wants you to leave that man.

MRS. JACKSON: No! He don't want that!
(Smothered giggles among the women.)

MARGARET: No, children, don't you be laughing this morning. This is serious business. The Lord, He got a road for each and every one of us to travel and we is got to be saying amen to Him, no matter what sorrow He cause us to bear. *(To* MRS. JACKSON*)* Don't let the Lord have to take another baby from you before you ready to do His will. Hand that child to me.
(Takes the child from MRS. JACKSON'S *arms.)*

SISTER MOORE: Kneel down, daughter. Kneel down there in front of the altar.
*(*MRS. JACKSON *kneels.)*

MARGARET: I want every soul under the sound of my voice to bow his head and pray silently with me as I pray.

(They bow their heads. MARGARET *stands, the child in her arms, head uplifted, and congregation begins to hum "Deep River.")*

Dear Lord, we come before you this morning to ask you to look down and bless this woman and her baby. Touch his little body, Lord, and heal him and drive out them tormenting demons. Raise him up, Lord, and make him a good man and a comfort to his mother. Yes, we know you can do it, Lord. You told us if we'd just call, trusting in your promise, you'd be sure to answer. And all these blessings we ask in the name of the Father—

ALL: In the name of the Father—

MARGARET: And in the name of the Son—

ALL: And in the name of the Son—

MARGARET: And in the name of the blessed Holy Ghost—

ALL: And in the name of the blessed Holy Ghost—

MARGARET: Amen.

ALL: Amen.

MARGARET *(Returning the child)*: God bless you, daughter. You go your way and trust the Lord. That child's going to be all right.

MRS. JACKSON: Thank you, sister. I can't tell you how much I thank you.

MARGARET: You ain't got me to thank. You come by here and let us know that child's all right, that's what'll please the Lord.

MRS. JACKSON: Yes. I sure will do that.

MARGARET: And bring your husband with you. You bring your *husband* with you.

MRS. JACKSON: Yes, sister. I'll bring him.

MARGARET: Amen!

(MRS. JACKSON *returns to her seat.* MARGARET *looks at her watch, motions to* ODESSA, *who rises and leaves. In a moment, we see her in the apartment. She exits through* LUKE's *room, returns a moment later without her robe, puts coffee on the stove, begins working.*)

(SISTER MOORE *comes forward.*)

SISTER MOORE: Well now, children, without no more ado, we's going to raise the sacrifice offering. And when I say sacrifice, I *mean* sacrifice. Boxer, hand me that basket.

(BROTHER BOXER *does so.* SISTER MOORE *holds a dollar up before the congregation and drops it in the plate.*)

I know you don't intend to see our pastor walk to Philadelphia. I want every soul in this congregation to drop just as much money in the plate as I just dropped, or *more*, to help with the cost of this trip. Go on, Brother Boxer, they going to give it to you, I know they is.

(*The congregation, which has been humming throughout all this, begins singing slightly more strongly as* BROTHER BOXER *passes around the plate, beginning at the back of the church.*)

ALL:

Glory, glory, hallelujah, since I laid my burdens down,
Glory, glory, hallelujah, since I laid my burdens down,
I feel better, so much better, since I laid my burdens down,
I feel better, so much better, since I laid my burdens down,
Glory, glory, hallelujah, since I laid my burdens down.

(MARGARET *leaves the pulpit and comes downstairs. The lights dim in the church; the music continues, but lower, and the offering is raised in pantomime.*)

ODESSA: Well! My sister sure walked around Zion this morning! (MARGARET *sits at the table.* ODESSA *pours coffee, begins preparing something for* MARGARET *to eat.*)

MARGARET: It ain't me, sister, it's the Holy Ghost. Odessa—? I been thinking I might take David with me to Philadelphia.

ODESSA: What you want to take him up there for? Who's going to play for the service down here?

MARGARET: Well, old Sister Price, she can sort of stand by—

ODESSA: She *been* standing by—but she sure can't play no piano, not for me she can't. She just ain't got no *juices,* somehow. When that woman is on the piano, the service just gets so dead you'd think you was in a Baptist church.

MARGARET: I'd like Mother Phillips to see what a fine, saved young man he turned out to be. It'll make her feel good. She told me I was going to have a hard time raising him—by myself.

(*Service is over, people are standing about chatting and slowly drifting out of the church.*)

ODESSA: Well, if he want to go—

MARGARET: David's got his first time to disobey me. The Word say, Bring up a child in the way he should go, and when he is old he will not depart from it. Now. That's the Word. (*At the suitcase*) Oh Lord, I sure don't feel like wasting no more time on Brother Boxer. He's a right sorry figure of a man, you know that?

ODESSA: I hope the Lord will forgive me, but, declare, I just can't help wondering sometimes who's on top in that holy marriage bed.

MARGARET (*Laughs*): Odessa!

ODESSA: Don't waste no time on him. He knows he ain't got no right to be driving a liquor truck.

MARGARET: Now, what do you suppose is happened to David? He should be here.

ODESSA: He's probably been cornered by some of the sisters. They's always pulling on him.

MARGARET: I praise my Redeemer that I got him raised right—even though I didn't have no man—you think David missed Luke?

(DAVID *enters the apartment.*)

Ah, there you are.

DAVID: Morning, Aunt Odessa. Morning, Mama. My! You two look —almost like two young girls this morning.

ODESSA: That's just exactly the way he comes on with the sisters. I reckon you know what you doing, taking him to Philadelphia.

DAVID: No, I mean it—just for a minute there. You both looked— different. Somehow—what about Philadelphia?

MARGARET: I was just asking your Aunt Odessa if she'd mind me taking you with me.

DAVID: Mama, I don't want to go to Philadelphia. Anyway—who's going to play for the service down here?

ODESSA: Sister Price can play for us.

DAVID: That woman can't play no piano.

MARGARET: Be careful how you speak about the saints, honey. God don't love us to speak no evil.

DAVID: Well, I'm sure she's sanctified and all that, but she *still* can't play piano. Not for *me*, she can't. She just makes me want to get up and leave the service.

MARGARET: Mother Phillips would just love to see you—

DAVID: I don't hardly remember Mother Phillips at all.

MARGARET: You don't remember Mother Phillips? The way you used to follow her around? Why, she used to spoil you something awful—you was always up in that woman's face—

when we—when we first come north—when Odessa was still working down home and we was living in Mother Phillips' house in Philadelphia. Don't you remember?

DAVID: Yeah. Sort of. But, Mama, I don't want to take a week off from music school.

MARGARET: Is the world going to fall down because you don't go to music school for a week?

DAVID: Well, Mama, music is just like everything else, you got to keep at it.

MARGARET: Well, you keeping at it. You playing in service all the time. I don't know what they can teach you in that school. You got a *natural* gift for music, David—(*A pause. They stare at each other*)—the Lord give it to you, you didn't learn it in no school.

DAVID: The Lord give me eyes, too, Mama, but I still had to go to school to learn how to read.

MARGARET: I don't know what's got into you lately, David.

DAVID: Well, Mama, I'm getting older. I'm not a little boy anymore.

MARGARET: I know you is getting older. But I hope you still got a mind stayed on the Lord.

DAVID: Sure. Sure, I have.

MARGARET: Where was you last night? You wasn't out to tarry service and don't nobody know what time you come in.

DAVID: I had to go—downtown. We—having exams next week in music school and—I was studying with some guys I go to school with.

MARGARET: Till way late in the morning?

DAVID: Well—it's a pretty tough school.

MARGARET: I don't know why you couldn't have had them boys come up here to *your* house to study. Your friends is always welcome, David, you know that.

DAVID: Well, this guy's got a piano in his house—it was more convenient.

(BROTHER *and* SISTER BOXER *and* SISTER MOORE *leave the church and start downstairs. The church dims out.*)

MARGARET: And what's wrong with that piano upstairs?

DAVID: Mama, I can't practice on that piano—

MARGARET: You can use that piano anytime you want to—

DAVID: Well, I couldn't have used it last night!
(*The* BOXERS *and* SISTER MOORE *enter.* DAVID *turns away.*)

SISTER MOORE: I come down here to tell Sister Margaret **myself** how she blessed my soul this morning! Praise the Lord, Brother David. How you feel this morning?

DAVID: Praise the Lord.

SISTER BOXER: Your mother sure preached a sermon this morning.

BROTHER BOXER: Did my heart good, amen. Did my heart *good.* Sister Odessa, what you got cool to drink in that fine new Frigidaire? (*Opens the Frigidaire*) You got any Kool-aid?

SISTER BOXER: You know you ain't supposed to be rummaging around in folks' iceboxes, Joel.

BROTHER BOXER: This ain't no icebox, this is a *Frigidaire.* Westinghouse. Amen! You don't mind my making myself at home, do you, Sister Odessa?

MARGARET: Just make yourself at home, Brother Boxer. I got to get ready to go. David, you better start packing—don't you make me late. He got any clean shirts, Odessa?

ODESSA: I believe so—I ironed a couple last night—he uses them up so fast.

SISTER MOORE: Why, is you going to Philadelphia with your mother, son? Why, that's just lovely!

DAVID: Mama—I got something else to do—this week—

MARGARET: You better hurry.
(DAVID *goes into* LUKE's *bedroom, pulls a suitcase from under the bed.*)

BROTHER BOXER: I believe David's sweet on one of them young
sisters in Philadelphia, that's why he's so anxious to go.
(DAVID *re-enters the kitchen.*) How about it, boy? You got
your eye on one of them Philadelphia saints? One of them
young ones?

MARGARET: David's just coming up with me because I asked him
to come and help me.

SISTER MOORE: Praise the Lord. That's sweet. The Lord's going to
bless you, you hear me, David?

BROTHER BOXER: Ain't many young men in the Lord like David.
I got to hand it to you, boy. I been keeping my eye on you
and you is—all right!
(*He claps* DAVID *on the shoulder.*)

SISTER BOXER: How long you figure on being gone, Sister Margaret?

MARGARET: I ain't going to be gone no longer than I have to—this
is a mighty sad journey. I don't believe poor Mother Phillips
is long for this world. And the way her congregation's behaving—it's just enough to make you weep.

ODESSA: I don't know what's got into them folks up there, cutting
up like they is, and talking about the Lord's anointed. I
guess I *do* know what's got into them, too—ain't nothing but
the Devil. You know, we is really got to watch and pray.

SISTER MOORE: They got more nerve than I got. You ain't never
going to hear me say nothing against them the Lord is set
above me. No sir. That's just asking for the wrath.

ODESSA: It'll fall *on* you, too. You all is seen the way the Lord is
worked with Sister Margaret right here in this little taber-
nacle. You remember all those people tried to set themselves
up against her—? Where is they now? The Lord is just let
every one of them be dispersed.

SISTER BOXER: Even poor little Elder King is in his grave.

BROTHER BOXER: I sort of liked old Elder King. The Lord moved
him right out just the same.

SISTER MOORE: He'd done got too *high*. He was too set in his ways. All that talk about not wanting women to preach. He didn't want women to do nothing but just sit quiet.

MARGARET: But I remember, Sister Moore, you wasn't so much on women preachers, neither, when I first come around.

SISTER MOORE: The Lord opened my eyes, honey. He opened my eyes the first time I heard you preach. Of course, I ain't saying that Elder King couldn't preach a sermon when the power was on him. And it *was* under Elder King that I come into the church.

BROTHER BOXER: You weren't sweet on Elder King, were you, Sister Moore?

SISTER MOORE: I ain't never been sweet on no man but the Lord Jesus Christ.

SISTER BOXER: You remember Elder King, son? You weren't nothing but a little bundle in them days.

DAVID: I was reading and writing already. I was even playing the piano already. It was him had this church then and we was living down the block.

BROTHER BOXER: I reckon you must have missed your daddy sometimes, didn't you, son?

SISTER MOORE: If he'd stayed around his daddy, I guarantee you David wouldn't be the fine, saved young man he is today, playing piano in church, would you, boy?

DAVID: No'm, I reckon I wouldn't. Mama, if I'm going to be gone a whole week, there is something I've got to—

BROTHER BOXER: He better off without the kind of daddy who'd just run off and leave his wife and kid to get along the best they could. That ain't right. I believe in a man doing *right*, amen!

MARGARET: You hear him, don't you? *He* know—miss his daddy?

The Lord, He give me strength to be mother and daddy both. Odessa, you want to help me with my hair?
(*They start out.*)

DAVID: Mama—!

MARGARET: What is it, son?

DAVID: There is something I got to get down the block. I got to run down the block for a minute.

MARGARET: Can't it wait till you come back?

DAVID: No. I want to—borrow a music score from somebody. I can study it while I'm away.

MARGARET: Well, you hurry. We ain't got much time. You put something on. You act like you catching cold.
(ODESSA *and* MARGARET *exit through* LUKE's *room.*)

BROTHER BOXER: You got to say goodbye to some little girl down the block?

DAVID: I'll be right back.
(*He rushes into the street, vanishes in the alley.*)

BROTHER BOXER: Hmmph! I wonder what kind of business he got down the block. I guarantee you one thing—it ain't sanctified business.

SISTER BOXER: The Word say we ain't supposed to think no evil, Joel.

BROTHER BOXER: I got news for you folks. You know what I heard last night?

SISTER BOXER: Don't you come on with no more foolishness, Joel. I'm too upset. I can't stand it this morning.

SISTER MOORE: Don't you be upset, sugar. Everything's going to turn out all right—what did you hear, Brother Boxer?

BROTHER BOXER: That boy's daddy is back in New York. He's working in a jazz club downtown.

SISTER MORE: A *jazz* club?

SISTER BOXER: How come you know all this?

BROTHER BOXER: Heard it on the job, honey. God don't want us to be ignorant. He want us to know what's going on around us.

SISTER MOORE: Do Sister Margaret know this?

BROTHER BOXER: I bet you David, *he* know it—he been keeping bad company. Some young white boy, didn't have nothing better to do, went down yonder and drug his daddy up to New York—for a comeback. Last time anybody heard about him, he was real sick with TB. Everybody thought he was dead.

SISTER MOORE: Poor Sister Margaret! A jazz club!

SISTER BOXER: Poor Sister Margaret! She ain't as poor as I am.

BROTHER BOXER: You ain't poor, sugar. You got me. And I ain't going to stay poor forever.

SISTER MOORE: I'm going to talk to her about that job business now. She reasonable. She'll listen.

SISTER BOXER: She ain't going to listen.

SISTER MOORE: Of course she's going to listen. Folks is got a right to make a living.

BROTHER BOXER: Uh-huh. Folks like us ain't got nothing and ain't never supposed to have nothing. We's supposed to live on the joy of the Lord.

SISTER MOORE: It ain't like Brother Boxer was going to become a drunkard or something like that—he won't even *see* the liquor—

SISTER BOXER: He won't even be selling it.

SISTER MOORE: He just going to be driving a truck around the city, doing hard work. I declare, I don't see nothing wrong with that.

SISTER BOXER: Sister Moore, you know that woman I work for, sometime she give a party and I got to serve them people cocktails. I *got* to. Now, I don't believe the Lord's going to punish me just because I'm working by the sweat of my brow the only way I *can*. He say, "Be in the world but not of it." But you got to be *in* it, don't care how holy you get, you got to *eat*.

BROTHER BOXER: I'm glad Sister Boxer mentioned it to you, Sister Moore. I wasn't going to mention it to you myself because I was sure you'd just take Sister Margaret's side against us.

SISTER MOORE: Ain't no taking of sides in the Lord, Brother Boxer. I'm on the Lord's side. We is all sinners, saved by grace. Hallelujah!

(MARGARET *and* ODESSA *re-enter. The* BOXERS *and* SISTER MOORE *begin to sing.*)

SISTER MOORE:

What a mighty God we serve!

SISTER *and* BROTHER BOXER:

What a mighty God we serve!

TOGETHER:

Angels around the throne,

'Round the throne of God,

Crying, what a mighty God we serve!

MARGARET: Bless your hearts, children, that sure done my spirit good. You all ain't like them wayward children up in Philadelphia. It sure is nice to be here with my real faithful children.

(DAVID *enters the alley, slowly, looking back; enters the apartment.*)

BROTHER BOXER: Oh, we's faithful, Sister Margaret.

(*Jazz version of "Luke's Theme" begins.*)

SISTER MOORE: Yes, I'm mighty glad you said that, Sister Margaret. I'm mighty glad you *knows* that. Because the Lord's done laid something on my heart to say to you, right here and now, and you going to take it in the proper spirit, I know you is. I know you know I ain't trying to find fault. Old Sister Moore don't mean no wrong.

MARGARET: What is it, Sister Moore?

DAVID: Mama, can I see you for a minute?

MARGARET: In a minute, son.

SISTER MOORE: Why, Brother and Sister Boxer here, they just happened to mention to me something about this job you don't think Brother Boxer ought to take. I don't mean no wrong, Sister Margaret, and I know you the pastor and is set above me, but I'm an older woman than you are and, I declare, I don't see no harm in it.

MARGARET: You don't see no harm in it, Sister Moore, because the Lord ain't placed you where he's placed me. Ain't no age in the Lord, Sister Moore—older or younger ain't got a thing to do with it. You just remember that I'm your pastor.

SISTER MOORE: But, Sister Margaret, can't be no harm in a man trying to do his best for his family.

MARGARET: The Lord comes before all things, Sister Moore. All things. Brother Boxer's supposed to do his best for the Lord.

SISTER MOORE: But, Sister Margaret—

MARGARET: I don't want to hear no more about it.

(SISTERS MOORE *and* BOXER *exchange a bitter look and they begin singing a church tune.* ODESSA *closes* MARGARET's *suitcase and puts it on the floor.* LUKE *appears in the alley, walking very slowly.*)

SISTERS MOORE AND BOXER:

'Bye and 'bye when the morning comes
All the saints of God are gathering home,
We will tell the story how we overcome,
And we'll understand it better 'bye and 'bye.

(LUKE *climbs the stairs into the church, walks through it
slowly; finally enters the apartment as they finish the song.*)

LUKE: Good morning, folks.

(*Silence. Everyone stares, first at* LUKE, *then at* MARGARET.
MARGARET *stands perfectly still.*)

Maggie, you ain't hardly changed a bit. You *still* the prettiest
woman I ever laid eyes on.

MARGARET: Luke.

LUKE: Don't look at me like that. I changed that much? Well, sure,
I might of lost a little weight. But you gained some. You
ever notice how men, they tend to lose weight in later life,
while the women, they gain? You look good, Maggie. It's
good to see you.

MARGARET: Luke—

LUKE (*To* ODESSA): Hey, you look good too. It's mighty good to see
you again. You didn't think I'd come to New York and not
find you? Ain't you going to say nothing, neither?

ODESSA: Ah. You bad boy.

LUKE: I bet my son is in this room somewhere. He's got to be in
this room somewhere—(*To* BROTHER BOXER)—but I reckon
it can't be you. I know it ain't been that long. (*To* DAVID)
You come downtown last night to hear me play, didn't you?

DAVID: Yes. Yes, sir. I did.

LUKE: Why didn't you come up and say hello? I saw you, sitting
way in the back, way at the end of the bar. I knew right
away it was you. And, time I was finished, you was gone.
(*A pause*) Cat got your tongue, Maggie? (*To* DAVID) I never
knowed that to happen to your mama before.

MARGARET: I never knowed my son to lie to me, neither. God don't
like liars.

DAVID: I was going to tell you.

MARGARET: Luke, how'd you find us?

LUKE: I had to find you. I didn't come to cause you no trouble. I just come by to say hello.

ODESSA: Luke, sit down! I can't get over seeing you, right here in this room. I can't get over it. I didn't reckon on never seeing you no more—

LUKE: In life. I didn't neither. But here I am—

ODESSA: With your big, black, no-count self. You hungry?

LUKE: Odessa, you ain't never going to change. Everytime you see a man, you think you got to go digging for some pork chops. No, I ain't hungry. I'm tired, though. I believe I'll sit down. (*He sits.* ODESSA *and* DAVID *glance at each other quickly.*)

MARGARET: How long you going to be in New York, Luke? When did you get here? Nobody told me—(*She looks at* DAVID)—nobody told me—you was here—

LUKE: A couple of weeks is all. I figured I'd find you somewhere near a church. And you a pastor now? Well, I guess it suits you. She a good pastor?

SISTER MOORE: Amen!

LUKE: What do you think, David? (DAVID *is silent.*) Well, she sure used to keep on at me about my soul. Didn't you, Maggie? Of course, that was only toward the end, when things got to be so rough. In the beginning—well, it's always different in the beginning.

MARGARET: You ain't changed, have you? You still got the same carnal grin, that same carnal mind—you ain't changed a bit.

LUKE: People don't change much, Maggie—

MARGARET: Not unless the Lord changes their hearts—

LUKE: You ain't changed much, neither—you dress a little different.

MARGARET: Why did you come here? You ain't never brought me nothing but trouble, you come to bring me more trouble? Luke—I'm glad to see you and all but—I got to be going

28

away this afternoon. I stay busy all the time around this church. David, he stays busy too—and he's coming with me this afternoon.

LUKE: Well, honey, I'm used to your going. I done had ten years to get used to it. But, David—David, you can find a couple of minutes for your old man, can't you? Maybe you'd like to come out with me sometime—we could try to get acquainted—

DAVID: You ain't wanted to get acquainted all this time—

LUKE: Yes, I did. It ain't my fault—at least it ain't *all* my fault—that we ain't acquainted.

ODESSA: Luke!

DAVID: You run off and left us.

LUKE: Boy, your daddy's done a lot of things he's ashamed of, but I wouldn't never of run off and left you and your mother. Your mama knows that. (*A pause*) You tell him, Maggie. Who left? Did I leave you or did you leave me?

MARGARET: It don't make no difference now.

LUKE: Who left? Tell him.

MARGARET: When we was living with you, I didn't know half the time if I had a husband or not, this boy didn't know if he had a father!

LUKE: That's a goddam lie. *You* knew you had a husband—this boy knew he had a father. Who left the house—who left?

MARGARET: You was always on the road with them no-count jazz players—

LUKE: But who *left*?

MARGARET: I ain't going to stand here arguing with you—I got to go —David—

LUKE: *Who left?*

MARGARET: *I* did! *I* left! To get away from the stink of whisky—to save my baby—to find the Lord!

29

LUKE: I wouldn't never of left you, son. Never. Never in this world.

MARGARET: Leave us alone, Luke. Go away and leave us alone. I'm doing the Lord's work now—

DAVID: Mama—you just said—God don't like liars.

MARGARET: Your daddy weren't hardly ever home. I was going to explain it all to you—when you got big.

LUKE: I done spent ten years wishing you'd leave the Lord's work to the Lord. (*He rises slowly.*) You know where I'm working, boy. Come on down and see me. Please come on down and see me.

MARGARET: Luke, he ain't going down there. You want to see him, you come on up here.

LUKE: He's big enough to find his way downtown.

MARGARET: I don't want him hanging around downtown.

LUKE: It ain't no worse down there than it is up here.

MARGARET: I ain't going to fight with you—not now—in front of the whole congregation. Brother Boxer, call me a taxi. David, close that suitcase and get yourself a coat. We got to go.

(BROTHER BOXER *hesitates, rises, leaves.*)

ODESSA: Maggie, he's sick.

(LUKE *sways, falls against the table.* SISTER BOXER *screams.* DAVID *and* ODESSA *struggle to raise him.*)

SISTER MOORE: Try to get him back here in this little room. Back here, in this bed, in this little room.

(DAVID *and the women struggle with* LUKE *and get him to the bed.* DAVID *loosens his father's collar and takes off his shoes.*)

LUKE (*Moans*): Maggie.

SISTER BOXER: We better send that man to a hospital.

MARGARET: This here's a Holy Ghost station. The Lord don't do nothing without a purpose. Maybe the Lord wants to save his soul.

SISTER MOORE: Well, amen.

MARGARET: And Luke, if he want to keep on being hardhearted against the Lord, his blood can't be required at our hands. I got to go.

DAVID: Mama, I'm going to stay here. (*A pause*) Mama, couldn't you write or telephone or something and let them folks know you can't get up there right now?

SISTER BOXER: Yes, Sister Margaret, couldn't you do that? I don't believe that man is long for this world.

SISTER MOORE: Yes, Sister Margaret, everybody understands that when you got trouble in the home, the home comes first. Send a deputy up there. I'll go for you.

MARGARET: In this home, Sister Moore, the Lord comes first. The Lord made me leave that man in there a long time ago because he was a sinner. And the Lord ain't told me to stop doing my work just because he's come the way all sinners come.

DAVID: But, Mama, he's been calling you, he going to keep on calling you! What we going to do if he start calling for you again?

MARGARET: Tell him to call on the Lord! It ain't me can save him, ain't nothing but the Lord can save him!

ODESSA: But you might be able to help him, Maggie—if you was here.

DAVID: Mama, you don't know. You don't know if he be living, time you get back. (*The taxi horn is heard.*) But I reckon you don't care, do you?

MARGARET: Don't talk to your mother that way, son. I don't want to go. I got to go.

SISTER BOXER: When a woman make a vow to God, she got to keep it.

MARGARET: You folks do what you can for him, pray and hold onto God for him. *(To* ODESSA*)* You send me a telegram if—if anything happens. *(To the others)* You folks got a evening service to get through. Don't you reckon you better run, get a bite to eat, so you can get back here on time?

BROTHER BOXER *(Off stage)*: Sister Margaret!

MARGARET: Go, do like I tell you. David, see if you can find a doctor. You ain't going to do no good, standing there like that. Praise the Lord.

ODESSA: Praise the Lord.

MARGARET *(To the others, dangerously)*: Praise the Lord, I say.

SISTERS MOORE *and* BOXER *(Dry)*: Praise the Lord. (MARGARET *goes through the church into the street.)*

LUKE: Maggie. Maggie. Oh, Maggie.

ODESSA: Children, let us pray.

(Slowly, all, except DAVID, *go to their knees. They begin singing.)*

If Jesus had to pray, what about me?
If Jesus had to pray, what about me?
He had to fall down on His knees,
Crying Father, help me if you please,
If Jesus had to pray, what about me?

In the garden Jesus prayed
While night was falling fast.
He said Father, if you will,
Let this bitter cup be past

But if not I am content,
Let my will be lost in Thine.
If Jesus had to pray, what about me?

Curtain

END OF ACT ONE

ACT II

Late afternoon the following Saturday. The sun is bright-red, the street is noisy. Cries of children playing, blaring radios and jukeboxes, etc.

LUKE's room is dark, the shades drawn. He is still.

ODESSA, SISTER BOXER and SISTER MOORE are in the kitchen.

SISTER MOORE (*To* ODESSA): We all loves Sister Margaret, sugar, just as much as you do. But we's supposed to bear witness, amen, to the truth. Don't care *who* it cuts.

SISTER BOXER: She been going around all these years acting so *pure*.

SISTER MOORE: Sister Margaret ain't nothing but flesh and blood, like all the rest of us. And she is got to watch and pray— like all the rest of us.

ODESSA: Lord, honey, Sister Margaret, *she* know that.

SISTER BOXER: She don't act like she know it. She act like she way above all human trouble. She always up there on that mountain, don't you know, just a-chewing the fat with the Lord.

SISTER MOORE: That poor man!

ODESSA: Sister Moore, you ain't never had no use for men all your life long. Now, how come you sitting up here this afternoon, talking about that *poor* man and talking against your pastor?

SISTER MOORE: Don't you try to put words in my mouth, Sister Odessa, don't you do it! I ain't talking against my pastor, no, I ain't. I ain't doing a thing but talking like a Christian.

SISTER BOXER: Last Sunday she acted like she didn't think that man was good enough to touch the hem of that white robe of her'n. And, you know, that ain't no way to treat a man who knowed one *time* what you was like with no robe on.

SISTER MOORE: Sister Boxer!

35

SISTER BOXER: Well, it's the truth. I'm bearing witness to the truth. I reckon I always thought of Sister Margaret like she'd been born holy. Like she hadn't never been a young girl or nothing and hadn't never had no real temptations.

(BROTHER BOXER *enters.*)

ODESSA: I don't know how you could of thought that when everybody knowed she's been married—and she had a son.

BROTHER BOXER: Praise the Lord, holy sisters, can a man come in?

ODESSA: Come on in the house, Brother Boxer. (*To the others*) You be careful how you talk about your sister. The Lord ain't *yet* taken away His protecting arm.

BROTHER BOXER: Look like it might rain this evening.

ODESSA: Yes. The sky is getting mighty low.

SISTER BOXER: Oh, sure, I knowed she'd been married and she had this boy. But, I declare, I thought that that was just a mistake and she couldn't wait to get away from her husband. There's women like that, you know, ain't got much nature to them somehow.

SISTER MOORE: Now, you be careful, Sister Boxer, you know I ain't never been married, nor (*proudly*) I ain't never knowed no man.

SISTER BOXER: Well, it's different with you, Sister Moore. You give your life to the Lord right quick and you ain't got nothing like that to remember. But, you take me now, I'm a married woman and the Lord done blessed me with a real womanly nature and, I tell you, honey, you been married once, it ain't so easy to get along single. 'Course, I know the Holy Ghost is mighty and *will* keep—but, I declare, I wouldn't like to try it. No *wonder* that woman make so much noise when she get up in the pulpit.

BROTHER BOXER: She done gone too far, she done rose too *high*.

She done forgot it ain't the woman supposed to lead, it's the man.

ODESSA: Is you done forgot your salvation? Don't you know if she'd followed that man, he might have led her straight on down to hell?

SISTER BOXER: That ain't by no means certain. If she'd done her duty like a wife, she might have been able to lead that man right straight to the throne of grace. I led *my* man there.

BROTHER BOXER: Well, you's a woman, sugar, and, quite natural, you want your man to come to heaven. But I believe in Sister Margaret's heaven, ain't going to be no men allowed. When that young woman come to the altar last Sunday morning, wanted the saints to pray for her baby, the first words out of Sister Margaret's mouth was "You better leave your husband."

SISTER BOXER: Amen! The *first* words.

ODESSA: Children, you better be careful what you say about a woman ain't been doing nothing but trying to serve the Lord.

SISTER MOORE: Is she been trying to serve the Lord? Or is she just wanted to put herself up over everybody else?

BROTHER BOXER: Now, that's what I'm talking about. The Word say, You going to know a tree by its fruit. And we ain't been seeing such good fruit from Sister Margaret. I want to know, how come she think she can rule a church when she can't rule her own house? That husband of hers is in there, dying in his sins, and that half-grown, hypocrite son of hers is just running all roads to hell.

ODESSA: Little David's just been a little upset. He ain't thinking about going back into the world, he see what sin done for his daddy.

BROTHER BOXER: I got news for you, Sister Odessa. Little David ain't so little no more. I stood right in this very room last

Sunday when we found out that boy had been lying to his mother. That's *right*. He been going out to *bars*. And just this very evening, not *five* minutes ago, I seen him down on 125th Street with some white horn player—the one he say he go to *school* with—and two other boys and three girls. Yes sir. They was just getting into a car.

ODESSA: It's just natural for David to be seeing folks his own age every now and then. And they just might be fixing to drop him at this very doorstep, you don't know. He might be here in time for tarry service.

BROTHER BOXER: I don't hear no cars drawing up in front of this door—no, I don't. And I bet you prayer meeting ain't what David had on his mind. That boy had a cigarette between his lips and had his hand on one of them girls, a real common-looking, black little thing, he had his hand on her—well, like he knowed her pretty *well* and wasn't expecting her to send him off to no prayer meeting.

SISTER MOORE: The Lord sure has been causing the scales to fall from the eyes of His servant this week. Thank you, Jesus!

ODESSA: You ought to be ashamed of yourselves! You ought to be ashamed of your black, deceitful hearts. You's liars, every one of you, and the truth's not in you! (*A pause*) Brother Boxer, Sister Boxer, Sister Moore. Let's go upstairs and pray.

SISTER MOORE: Yes, we *better* go upstairs and pray. The Lord's been working in the hearts of some other folks in this church and they's going to be along presently, asking the elders of this church to give them an accounting—amen!—of their spiritual leader.

ODESSA: What kind of accounting, Sister Moore?

SISTER MOORE: Well, I just happened to be talking to some of the saints the other day and while we was talking some of them got to wondering just how much it cost to get to Philadelphia. Well, I said I didn't know because the Lord, He keep *me* close to home. But I said it couldn't cost but *so* much, ain't like she was going on a great long trip. Well—we got to talking about other things and then we just decided we'd come to church this evening and put our minds together. Amen. And let everybody say his piece and see how the Lord, *He* wanted us to move.

ODESSA: Was you there, too, Brother Boxer?

BROTHER BOXER: Naturally I was there too. I'm one of the elders of the church.

ODESSA: I'm one of the elders, too. But *I* wasn't there—wherever it was.

SISTER MOORE: We wasn't planning to shut you out, Sister Odessa. Some folks just happened to drop by the house and we got to talking. That's all.

ODESSA: Is folks thinking that Margaret's stealing their money?

SISTER BOXER: That ain't no way to talk, Sister Odessa. Before God, ain't nobody said a word about stealing.

SISTER MOORE: Ain't nobody accusing Margaret of *nothing*. Don't you let the Devil put that idea in your mind. Sister Margaret's been blessed with a real faithful congregation. Folks just loves Sister Margaret. Just the other day one of the saints—was it you, Sister Boxer?—one of the saints was saying to me how much trouble she have with her old refrigerator and she say it sure done her heart good to know her pastor had a nice, new frigidaire. Amen. She said it done her heart good.

(*They exit into the church. The lights go up slightly as they enter and sit. The church blacks out.*

For a moment the stage is empty. Then DAVID *appears, enters the house. He is very tired and nervous. He wanders about the kitchen; goes to* LUKE'S *room, looks in. He is about to turn away when* LUKE *speaks.*)

LUKE: Hello, there.

DAVID: I thought you was asleep.

LUKE: I ain't sleepy. Is it nighttime yet?

DAVID: No, not yet.

LUKE: Look like it's always nighttime in this room. You want to come in, pull up the shade for me?

(DAVID *does so. A faint sound of singing is heard from the church upstairs.*)

LUKE: Ain't you going to play piano for them tonight?

DAVID: I don't much feel like playing piano right now.

(*He is flustered; reaches in his pocket, takes out a pack of cigarettes, realizes his mistake too late.*)

LUKE: Didn't know you was smoking already. Let's have a cigarette.

DAVID: You ain't suppose to be smoking. The doctor don't want you smoking.

LUKE: The doctor ain't here now.

(DAVID *gives* LUKE *a cigarette, lights it, after a moment lights one for himself.*)

DAVID: Look like you'd of had enough of smoking by now.

LUKE: Sit down. We got a minute.

(DAVID *sits on the hassock at the foot of* LUKE's *bed.*)

LUKE: Didn't I hear you playing piano one night this week?

DAVID: No.

LUKE: Boy, I'm sure I heard you playing *one* night—at the beginning of the service?

DAVID: Oh. Yes, I guess so. I didn't stay. How did you know it was me?

LUKE: You play piano like I dreamed you would.

DAVID: I been finding out lately you was pretty good. Mama never let us keep a phonograph. I just didn't never hear any of your records—until here lately. You was right up there with the best, Jellyroll Morton and Louis Armstrong and cats like that.

LUKE: You fixing to be a musician?

DAVID: No.

LUKE: Well, it ain't much of a profession for making money, that's the truth.

DAVID: There were guys who did.

LUKE: There were guys who didn't.

DAVID: You never come to look for us. Why?

LUKE: I started to. I wanted to. I thought of it lots of times.

DAVID: Why didn't you never do it? Did you think it was good riddance we was gone?

LUKE: I was hoping you wouldn't never think that, never.

DAVID: I wonder what you expected me to think. I remembered you, but couldn't never talk about you. I used to hear about you sometime, but I couldn't never say, That's my daddy. I was too ashamed. I remembered how you used to play for me sometimes. That was why I started playing the piano. I used to go to sleep dreaming about the way we'd play together one day, me with my piano and you with your trombone.

LUKE: David. David.

DAVID: You never come. You never come when you could do us some good. You come now, now when you can't do nobody any good. Every time I think about it, think about *you*, I want to break down and cry like a baby. You make me—ah! You make me feel so bad.

LUKE: Son—don't try to get away from the things that hurt you. The things that hurt you—sometimes that's all you got. You

41

got to learn to live with those things—and—use them. I've seen people—put themselves through terrible torture—and die—because they was afraid of getting hurt.

(*He wants to get rid of his cigarette.* DAVID *takes it from him. They stare at each other for a moment.*)

I used to hold you on my knee when you weren't nothing but a little—you didn't have no teeth then. Now I reckon you's already started to lose them. I reckon I thought we was a-going to bring down the moon, you and me, soon as you got a little bigger. I planned all kinds of things for you—they never come to pass.

DAVID: You ain't never been saved, like Mama. Have you?

LUKE: Nope.

DAVID: How come Mama, she got saved?

LUKE: I reckon she thought she better had—being married to me. I don't know. Your mama's kind of proud, you know, proud and silent. We had us a little trouble. And she wouldn't come to me. That's when she found the Lord.

DAVID: I remember. I remember—that was when the baby was born dead. And Mama was in the hospital—and you was drunk, going to that hospital all the time—and I used to hear you crying, late at night. *Did* she find the Lord?

LUKE: Can't nobody know but your mama, son.

DAVID: A few months ago some guys come in the church and they heard me playing piano and they kept coming back all the time. Mama said it was the Holy Ghost drawing them in. But it wasn't.

LUKE: It was your piano.

DAVID: Yes. And I didn't draw them in. They drew me out. They setting up a combo and they want me to come in with them. That's when I stopped praying. I really began to think about it hard. And, Daddy—things started happening inside me which hadn't ever happened before. It was terrible. It was wonderful. I started looking around this house, around this church—like I was seeing it for the first time. Daddy—that's when I stopped believing—it just went away. I got so I just hated going upstairs to that church. I hated coming home. I hated lying to Mama all the time—and—I knew I had to do something—and that's how—I was scared, I didn't know what to do. I didn't know how to stay here and I didn't know how to go—and—there wasn't anybody I could talk to—I couldn't do—nothing! Every time I—even when I tried to make it with a girl—something kept saying, Maybe this is a sin. I hated it! (*He is weeping.*) I made Mama let me go to music school and I started studying. I got me a little part-time job. I been studying for three months now. It gets better all the time—you know? I don't mean *me*—I got a long way to go—but *it* gets better. And I was trying to find some way of preparing Mama's mind—

LUKE: When you seen me. And you got to wondering all over again if you wanted to be like your daddy and end up like your daddy. Ain't that right?

DAVID: Yeah, I guess that's right.

LUKE: Well, son, tell you one thing. Wasn't music put me here. The most terrible time in a man's life, David, is when he's done lost everything that held him together—it's just gone and he can't find it. The whole world just get to be a great big empty basin. And it just as hollow as a basin when you strike it with your fist. Then that man start going down. If don't no hand reach out to help him, that man goes under. You know, David, it don't take much to hold a man together. A man can lose a whole lot, might look to everybody else that he done lost so much that he ought to want to be dead, but he can keep on—he can even die with his head up, hell, as long as he got that one thing. That one thing is *him*,

David, who he is inside—and, son, I don't believe no man ever got to that without somebody loved him. Somebody *looked* at him, looked *way* down in him and spied him way down there and showed him to himself—and then started pulling, a-pulling of him up—so he could live. *(Exhausted)* Hold your head up, David. You'll have a life. Tell me there's all kinds of ways for ruined men to keep on living. You hears about guys sometimes who got a bullet in their guts and keeps on running—running—spilling blood every inch, keeps running a long time—before they fall. I don't know what keeps them going. Faith—or something—something—something I never had. *(A pause)* So don't you think you got to end up like your daddy just because you want to join a band.

DAVID: Daddy—weren't the music enough?

LUKE: The music. The music. Music is a moment. But life's a long time. In that moment, when it's good, when you really swinging—then you joined to everything, to everybody, to skies and stars and every living thing. But music ain't kissing. Kissing's what you want to do. Music's what you *got* to do, *if* you got to do it. Question is how long you can keep up with the music when you ain't got nobody to kiss. You know, the music don't come out of the air, baby. It comes out of the man who's blowing it.

DAVID: You must have had a time.

LUKE: I had me a time all right.

DAVID: Didn't you never call on God?

LUKE: No. I figured it was just as much His fault as mine.

DAVID: Didn't you never get scared?

LUKE: Oh yes.

DAVID: But you're not scared now?

LUKE: Oh yes.

(DAVID *goes off, stage left. The lights come up in the church, dim down in the apartment.* SISTER MOORE, SISTER BOXER, BROTHER BOXER, *along with some members of the congregation seen in the First Act, are grouped together in camp chairs.* ODESSA *sits a little away from them.* SISTER RICE, *fortyish,* SISTER SALLY, *extremely young and voluptuous,* SISTER DOUGLASS, *quite old and slow and black.*)

SISTER SALLY: Why, a couple of months ago, just after we got married? Why, Herman and I, we had to go to Philadelphia *several* times and it don't cost no forty some odd dollars to get there. Why, it don't cost *that* much round trip.

SISTER DOUGLASS: It ain't but up the road a ways, is it? I used to go up there to see my nephew, he stay too busy to be able to get to New York much. It didn't seem to me it took so long. 'Course, I don't remember how much it cost.

ODESSA: I don't know why you folks don't just call up Pennsylvania Station and just *ask* how much it costs to get to Philadelphia.

BROTHER BOXER: Most folks don't go to Philadelphia by train, Sister Odessa. They takes the bus because the bus is cheaper.

SISTER MOORE: Now, of course ain't nothing these days what you might call really *cheap.* Brother Boxer, you remember when Sister Boxer had to go down home to bury her sister? You was going up to Philadelphia quite regular there for a while. You remember how much it cost?

SISTER BOXER: You ain't never mentioned you knew anybody in Philadelphia.

SISTER SALLY: Men don't never tell women nothing. Look like you always finding out something new.

BROTHER BOXER: Man better not tell a woman everything he know, not if he got good sense. (*To* SISTER MOORE) It didn't cost no more'n about three or four dollars.

SISTER BOXER: That round trip or one way?

SISTER DOUGLASS: How much you folks say you raised on the offering last Sunday?

SISTER MOORE: Brother Boxer and me, we counted it, and put it in the envelope. It come to—what did it come to altogether, Brother Boxer? Give us the *exact* figure, amen.

BROTHER BOXER: It come to forty-one dollars and eighty-seven cents.

SISTER RICE: Don't seem to me we ought to be sitting here like this, worrying about the few pennies we give our pastor last Sunday. We been doing it Sunday after Sunday and ain't nobody never had nothing to say against Sister Margaret. She's our pastor, we ain't supposed to be thinking no evil about her.

SISTER MOORE: That's what I say, amen. Sister Margaret our pastor and the few pennies we scrapes together by the sweat of our brow to give her she got a right to do with as she see *fit,* amen! And I think we ought to stop discussing it right here and now and just realize that we's blessed to have a woman like Sister Margaret for our shepherd.

ODESSA: You folks sound like a church don't have to pay no rent, and don't never pay no bills and nothing in a church don't never wear out. Them chairs you got your behinds on right now, they have to keep on being replaced—you folks is always breaking them during the service, when you gets happy. Those of you what wears glasses, though, I notice you don't never break them. You holds yourself together somehow until somebody comes and takes them off'n you. Rugs on the floor cost money, robes cost money—and you people is just murder on hymnbooks, tambourines and Bibles. Now, Margaret don't use hardly none of that money on herself—ain't enough money *in* this church for nobody to be able to live off it.

BROTHER BOXER: You folks got a new frigidaire, though. I ain't saying nothing, but—

ODESSA: That frigidaire is in *my* name, Brother Boxer—it's the first new thing I bought for that house in I don't know how many years—with money *I* made from scrubbing white folks' floors. Ain't a one of you put a penny in it. Now. You satisfied?

SISTER MOORE: How's your mother getting along, Sister Rice? I hope she feeling better. We ain't seen her for a long time.

SISTER RICE: We's holding onto God for her. But she been doing poorly, poor thing. She say she sure do miss not being able to come out to service.

SISTER MOORE: But Sister Margaret's been there, praying for her, ain't she?

SISTER RICE: No, Sister Margaret ain't got there yet. She say she was going to make it last Sunday, but then she had to go to Philadelphia—

SISTER MOORE: Poor Sister Margaret. She sure has had her hands full.

SISTER BOXER: She got her hands full right down there in her own house. Reckon she couldn't get over to pray for your mother, Sister Rice, she couldn't stay here to pray for her own husband.

SISTER DOUGLASS: The Word say we ain't supposed to think no evil, Sister Boxer. Sister Margaret have to go the way the Lord leads her.

SISTER BOXER: I ain't thinking no evil. But the Word *do* say, if you don't love your brother who you can see, how you going to love God, who you ain't seen?

SISTER SALLY: That is a *true* saying, bless the Lord.

SISTER DOUGLASS: How is that poor, sin-sick soul?

SISTER BOXER: He ain't long for this world. He lying down there, just rotten with sin. He dying in his sins.

SISTER MOORE: He real pitiful. I declare, when you see what sin can do it make you stop and think.

SISTER RICE: Do David spend much time with him, Sister Odessa? I reckon it must make him feel real bad to see his father lying there like that.

ODESSA: Luke so sick he do a lot of sleeping, so David can't really be with him so much.

SISTER DOUGLASS: Oh. We ain't seen David hardly at all this week and I just figured he was downstairs with his father.

BROTHER BOXER: Little David—I'm mighty afraid little David got other fish to fry. The Lord has allowed me to see, with my *own* eyes, how David's done started straying from the Word. I ain't going to say no more. But the brother needs prayer. Amen. Sister Moore, do you recollect how much it cost us to get that there window painted?

SISTER MOORE: Why, no, Brother Boxer, I don't. Seem to me it cost about fifty dollars.

SISTER BOXER: It cost fifty-three dollars. I remember because Sister Margaret weren't here when the work was finished and I give the man the money myself.

SISTER DOUGLASS: It a mighty pretty window. Look like it make you love Jesus even more, seeing Him there all in the light like that.

BROTHER BOXER: You remember who she got to do it?

SISTER BOXER: Why, she got one of them folks from Philadelphia to do it. That was before we was even affiliated with that church.

BROTHER BOXER: I believe we could of got it done for less, right down here among our own.

SISTER RICE: I don't know, Brother Boxer, that's fine work. You got to have *training* for that. People think you can just get up and draw a picture, but it ain't so.

SISTER DOUGLASS: That's the truth, Sister Rice. My nephew, he draws, and he all the time telling me how hard it is. I have to help him out all the time, you know, 'cause it ain't easy to make a living that way—

SISTER BOXER: I don't know why your nephew couldn't of drew it for us. I bet you he wouldn't of charged no fifty-three dollars, either.

SISTER SALLY: My mother, she go to Bishop William's church up there on 145th Street, you know, and she was saying to me just the other day she don't see why, after all these years, Sister Margaret couldn't move her congregation to a better building.

SISTER MOORE: Sister Margaret ain't worried about these buildings down here on earth, daughter. Sister Margaret's working on another building, hallelujah, in the *heavens*, not made with hands!

SISTER SALLY: Why, that's what my mother's doing, too, Sister Moore. But she say she don't see why you got to be in dirt all the time just because you a Christian.

ODESSA: If anybody in this church is in dirt, it ain't the dirt of this church they's in. I know this ain't no palace but it's the best we can do right now. Sister Margaret's been doing her best for every one of us and it ain't right for us to sit up here this evening, back-biting against her.

SISTER MOORE: Sister Odessa, I told you downstairs it ain't nothing but the Devil putting them thoughts in your head. Ain't nobody back-biting against your sister. We's just discussing things, the Lord, He give us eyes to see and understanding to understand.

SISTER BOXER: Amen!

SISTER MOORE: I got yet to say my first word against your sister. I know the Lord is seen fit, for reasons *I* ain't trying to discover, to burden your sister with a heavy burden. I ain't sitting in judgment. I ain't questioning the ways of the Lord. I don't know what that half-grown son of hers done seen to cause him to backslide this-a-way. *I* don't know why that man of hers is down there, dying in his sins—just rotting away, amen, before her eyes. I ain't asking no questions. I'm just waiting on the Lord because He say He'll reveal all things. In His own good time.

SISTER BOXER: Amen! And I believe He's going to use us to help him reveal.

(SISTER MOORE *begins singing.*)

ODESSA: Sister Moore!

SISTER MOORE:

You can run on for a long time,

You can run on for a long time,

You can run on for a long time,

I tell you the great God Almighty gonna cut you down.

CONTRALTO:

Some people go to church just to signify

Trying to make a date with their neighbor's wife.

Brother, let me tell you just as sure as you're born

You better leave that woman, leave her alone.

One of these days, just mark my word,

You'll think your neighbor has gone to work,

You'll walk right up and knock on the door—

That's all, brother, you'll knock no more.

Go tell that long-tongued liar, go tell that midnight rider,

Go tell the gambler, rambler, backslider,

Tell him God Almighty's gonna cut you down.

(During the last line of song MARGARET *enters.)*

MARGARET: Praise the Lord, children. I'm happy to see you's holding the fort for Jesus.

SISTER MOORE: Praise the *Lord*, Sister Margaret! We was just wondering if you was *ever* coming back here!

SISTER BOXER: Praise the Lord, Sister Margaret, we sure is glad you's back. Did you have a good trip?

MARGARET: Praise the Lord, children. It sure is good to be back here. The Lord, He give us the victory in Philadelphia, amen! He just worked and uncovered sin and put them children on their knees!

ALL:

What a wonder, what a marvel,
And I'm glad that I can tell
That the Lord saved me and He set me free,
He endowered me with power,
And gave me the victory.

What a wonder, what a marvel,
And I'm glad that I can tell
That the Lord saved me and He set me free,
He endowered me with power,
And gave me the victory.

What a wonder, what a marvel,
And I'm glad that I can tell
That the Lord saved me and He set me free,
He endowered me with power,
And gave me the victory.

SISTER MOORE: When it come time for the Lord to uncover, He sure do a mighty uncovering!

MARGARET *(To* ODESSA)*:* Has everything been all right, sugar?

ODESSA: Yes, Maggie. Everything's been fine.

SISTER BOXER: How did you come down, Sister Margaret? Did you take the train or the bus?

MARGARET: Honey, one of the Philadelphia saints drove me down.

SISTER BOXER: *Drove* you down! I reckon you *did* get the victory. *(Laughter.)*

SISTER MOORE: Well, bless the Lord, that's real nice. I reckon they was trying to help you cut down on expenses.

MARGARET: Children, tomorrow is going to be a mighty big Sunday. The Philadelphia church is coming down here, all of them, for the evening service. Even Mother Phillips might be coming, she say she's feeling so much better. You know, this church is going to be packed. *(To* BROTHER BOXER*)* Brother Boxer, you going to have to clear a little space around that piano because they bringing their drums down here. *(To the others)* They got drums up there, children, and it help the service a whole lot, I wouldn't have believed it. *(The merest pause)* They even got a man up there making a joyful noise to the Lord on a trumpet!

BROTHER BOXER: He coming down here, too?

MARGARET: Oh, yes, he'll be here. Children, I want you all to turn out in full force tomorrow and show them Philadelphia saints how to praise the Lord.

SISTER DOUGLASS: Look like they going to be able to teach us something, they got them drums and trumpets and all—

SISTER MOORE: That don't make no difference. We been praising the Lord without that all this time, we ain't going to let them show us up.

MARGARET: You better *not* let them show you up. You supposed to be an example to the *Philadelphia* church.

SISTER RICE: But, Sister Margaret, you think it's right to let them come down here with all that—with drums and trumpets? Don't that seem kind of worldly?

MARGARET: Well, the evil ain't in the drum, Sister Rice, nor yet in the trumpet. The evil is in what folks do with it and what it leads them to. Ain't no harm in praising the Lord with anything you get in your hands.

BROTHER BOXER: It'll bring Brother David out to church again, I guarantee you that. That boy loves music.

MARGARET: I hope you don't mean he loves music more than he loves the Lord.

BROTHER BOXER: Oh, we all know how much he loves the Lord. But he got trumpets or *some* kind of horn in his *blood*.

ODESSA: I reckon you going to have to speak to David, Maggie. He upset about his daddy and he ain't been out to service much this week.

SISTER MOORE: When you upset, that's the time to come to the Lord. If you believe He loves you, you got to trust His love.

MARGARET: Poor David. He don't talk much, but he feel a whole lot.

SISTER BOXER: How is his daddy, Sister Margaret? You been downstairs to look at him yet?

ODESSA: We ain't allowed to break his rest.

MARGARET: I pray the Lord will save his soul.

SISTER MOORE: Amen. And, church, we got to pray that the Lord will draw our David back to Him, so he won't end up like his daddy. Our pastor, she got a lot to bear.

MARGARET: David ain't foolish, Sister Moore, and he done been well raised. He ain't going back into the world.

SISTER MOORE: I hope and pray you's right, from the bottom of my soul I do. But every living soul needs prayer, Sister Margaret, every living soul. And we's just trying to hold up your hand in this time of trouble.

SISTER BOXER: Sister Margaret, I ain't trying to dig up things what buried. But you told Joel and me he couldn't take that job driving that truck. And now you bringing down drums and trumpets from Philadelphia because you say the evil ain't in the thing, it's in what you do with the thing. Well, ain't that truck a *thing*? And if it's all right to blow a trumpet in church, why ain't it all right for Joel to drive that truck, so he can contribute a little more to the house of God? This church is *poor*, Sister Margaret, we ain't got no cars to ride you around in, like them folks in Philadelphia. But do that mean we got to *stay* poor?

MARGARET: Sister Boxer, you know as well as me that there's many a piano out in them night clubs. But that ain't stopped us from using a piano in this church. And there's all the difference in the world between a saint of God playing music in a church and helping to draw people in and a saint of God spending the whole day driving a liquor truck around. Now I know you got good sense and I know you see that, and I done already told you I don't want to talk no more about it.

SISTER BOXER: It don't seem to me you's being fair, Sister Margaret.

MARGARET: When is I ain't been fair? I been doing my best, as the Lord led me, for all of you, for all these years. How come you to say I ain't been fair? You sound like you done forget your salvation, Sister Boxer.

(DAVID *reappears, carrying a phonograph and a record. He enters* LUKE's *bedroom.* LUKE's *eyes are closed. He goes to the bed and touches him lightly and* LUKE *opens his eyes.*)

LUKE: What you got there?

DAVID: You going to recognize it. Be quiet, listen.
(*He plugs in the phonograph.*)

SISTER MOORE: Now the Word say Blessed is the peacemaker, so let me make peace. This ain't no way to be behaving.

MARGARET: Sister Moore, I'm the pastor of this church and I don't appreciate you acting as though we was both in the wrong.

SISTER MOORE: Ain't nobody infallible, Sister Margaret. Ain't a soul been born infallible.

ODESSA: We better all fall on our knees and pray.

MARGARET: Amen.
(DAVID *has turned on the record, watching* LUKE. *The sound of* LUKE's *trombone fills the air.*)

SISTER MOORE: Where's that music coming from?

ODESSA: It must be coming from down the street.

MARGARET (*Recognition*): Oh, my God.

SISTER MOORE: It coming from your house, Sister Margaret.

MARGARET: Kneel down. (*They watch her*) Kneel *down,* I say!
(LUKE *takes his mouthpiece from his pajama pocket and pantomimes a phrase, then stops, his mouthpiece in his hand, staring at his son.*

In the church, slowly, they kneel.)

MARGARET: Pray. Every single one of you. Pray that God will give you a clean heart and a clean mind and teach you to obey. (*She turns and leaves the pulpit. Upstairs, they turn and look at each other and slowly rise from their knees. The church dims out.*

MARGARET *stands for a moment in the door of* LUKE's *bedroom.*)

MARGARET: David!

DAVID: Mama—I didn't hear you come in!

MARGARET: I reckon you didn't hear me come in. The way that box is going, you wouldn't of hear the Holy *Ghost* come in. Turn it off! Turn it off!
(DAVID *does so.*)

MARGARET: You ain't supposed to let your daddy come here and lead you away from the Word. You's supposed to lead your daddy to the Lord. (*To* LUKE) It seems to me by this time the very sound of a horn would make you to weep or pray.

DAVID: It's one of Daddy's old records. That you never let me play.

MARGARET: Where'd that box come from? What's it doing in this house?

DAVID: I borrowed it.

MARGARET: Where'd you get that record?

DAVID: It's mine.

LUKE: That's right. It's his—now.
(*A pause.*)

MARGARET: I ain't trying to be hard on you, son. But we's got to watch and pray. We's got to watch and pray.

DAVID: Yes, Mama. Mama, I got to go now.

MARGARET: Where you going, son?

LUKE: Maggie, he ain't five years old, he's eighteen. Let him alone.

MARGARET: You be quiet. You ain't got nothing to say in all this.

LUKE: That's a lie. I got a lot to say in all this. That's my son. Go on, boy. You remember what I told you.

DAVID: I'm taking the record player back where I got it. (*At the door*) So long—Daddy—

LUKE: Go on, boy. You all right?

MARGARET: David—

DAVID: I'm all right, Daddy.
(DAVID *goes.*)

LUKE: So long, son.

MARGARET: Luke, ain't you never going to learn to do right? Ain't you learned nothing out all these years, all this trouble?

LUKE: I done learned a few things. They might not be the same things you wanted me to learn. Hell, I don't know if they are the same things *I* wanted me to learn.

MARGARET: I ain't never wanted you to learn but one thing, the love of Jesus.

LUKE: You done changed your tune a whole lot. That ain't what we was trying to learn in the beginning.

MARGARET: The beginning is a long time ago. And weren't nothing but foolishness. Ain't nothing but the love of God can save your soul.

LUKE: Maggie, don't fight with me. I don't want to fight no more. We didn't get married because we loved God. We loved each other. Ain't that right?

MARGARET: I sure can't save your soul, Luke.

LUKE: There was a time when I believed you could.

MARGARET: Luke. That's all past. (*She sits on the edge of the bed.*) Luke, it been a long time we ain't seen each other, ten long years. Look how the Lord done let you fall. Ain't you ready to give up to Him and ask Him to save you from your sins and bring peace to your soul?

LUKE: Is you got peace in your soul, Maggie?

MARGARET: Yes! He done calmed the waters, He done beat back the powers of darkness, He done made me a new woman!

LUKE: Then that other woman—that funny, fast-talking, fiery little thing I used to hold in my arms—He done done away with her?

MARGARET (*Rises*): All that's—been burned out of me by the power of the Holy Ghost.

LUKE: Maggie, I remember you when you didn't hardly know if the Holy Ghost was something to drink or something to put on your hair. I know we can't go back, Maggie. But you mean that whole time we was together, even with all our trouble, you mean it don't mean nothing to you now? You mean— you don't remember? I was your *man*, Maggie, we was everything to each other, like that Bible of yours say, we was one flesh—we used to get on each other's nerves something *awful*—you mean that's all dead and gone?

MARGARET: You is still got that old, sinful Adam in you. You's thinking with Adam's mind. You don't understand that when the Lord changes you He makes you a new person and He gives you a new mind.

LUKE: Don't talk at me like I was a congregation. I ain't no con- gregation. I'm your husband, even if I ain't much good to you no more.

MARGARET: Well, if it's all dead and gone—you killed it! Don't you lay there and try to make me feel accused. If it's all dead and gone, you did it, you did it!

LUKE: Ah. Now we coming. At least it wasn't the Holy Ghost. Just how did I do it, Maggie? How did I kill it?

MARGARET: I never knew why you couldn't be like other men.

LUKE: I was the man you married, Maggie. I weren't supposed to be like other men. When we didn't have nothing, I made it my business to find something, didn't I? Little David always had shoes to his feet when I was there and you wasn't never

58

dressed in rags. And anyway—you want me to repent so you can get me into heaven, or you want me to repent so you can keep David home?

MARGARET: Is David been talking about leaving home?

LUKE: Don't you reckon he going to be leaving home one day?

MARGARET: David going to work with me in these here churches and he going to be a pastor when he get old enough.

LUKE: He got the call?

MARGARET: He'll *get* the call.

LUKE: You sure got a lot of influence with the Holy Ghost.

MARGARET: I didn't come in here to listen to you blaspheme. I just come in here to try to get you to think about your soul.

LUKE: Margaret, once you told me you loved me and then you jumped up and ran off from me like you couldn't stand the smell of me. What you think *that* done to my soul?

MARGARET: I had to go. The Lord told me to go. We'd been living like—like two animals, like two children, never thought of nothing but their own pleasure. In my heart, I always knew we couldn't go on like that—we was too happy—

LUKE: Ah!

MARGARET: And that winter—them was terrible days, Luke. When I'd almost done gone under, I heard a voice. The voice said, Maggie, you got to find you a hiding place. I knowed weren't no hiding place to be found in you—not in no man. And you—you cared more about that trombone than you ever cared about me!

LUKE: You ought to of tried me, Maggie. If you had trusted me till then, you ought to have trusted me a little further.

MARGARET: When they laid my baby in the churchyard, that poor little baby girl what hadn't never drawn breath, I knowed

59

if we kept on a-going the way we'd been going, He weren't going to have no mercy on neither one of us. And that's when I swore to my God I was going to change my way of living.

LUKE: Then that God you found—He just curse the poor? But He don't bother nobody else? Them big boys, them with all the money and all the manners, what let you drop dead in the streets, watch your blood run all over the gutters, just so they can make a lousy dime—He get along fine with them? What the hell had we done to be cursed, Maggie?

MARGARET: We hadn't never thought of nothing but ourself. We hadn't never thought on God!

LUKE: All we'd done to be cursed was to be *poor,* that's all. That's why little Margaret was laid in the churchyard. It was just because you hadn't never in your whole life had enough to eat and you was sick that winter and you didn't have no strength. Don't you come on with me about no judgment, Maggie. That was my baby, too.

MARGARET: *Your* baby, yours! I was the one who carried it in my belly, *I* was the one who felt it starving to death inside me. *I* was the one who had it, in the cold and dark alone! You wasn't nowhere to be found, you was out drunk.

LUKE: I was *there.* I was *there.* Yes, I was drunk, but I was sitting at your bedside every day. Every time you come to yourself you looked at me and started screaming about how I'd killed our baby. Like I'd taken little Margaret and strangled her with my own two hands. *Yes,* I was drunk but I was waiting for you to call me. You never did. You never did.

MARGARET: I reckon the Lord was working with me, even then.

LUKE: I reckon so.

MARGARET: Luke. Luke, it don't do to question God.

LUKE: No, it don't. It sure as hell don't.

MARGARET: Don't let your heart be bitter. You'd come way down, Luke, bitterness ain't going to help you now. Let Him break your heart, let the tears come, ask Him to forgive you for your sins, call on Him, call on Him!

LUKE: Call on Him for what, Maggie?

MARGARET: To save your soul. To keep you from the fires of hell. So we can be together in glory.

LUKE: I want to be together with you now.

MARGARET: Luke. You ain't fighting with men no more. You's fighting with God. You got to humble yourself, you got to bow your head.

LUKE: It ain't going to be like that, Maggie. I ain't going to come crawling to the Lord now, making out like I'd do better if I had it all to do over. I ain't going to go out, screaming against hell-fire. It would make *you* right. It would prove to David you was right. It would make me nothing but a dirty, drunk old man didn't do nothing but blow music and chase the women all his life. I ain't going to let it be like that. That ain't all there was to it. You know that ain't all there was to it.

MARGARET: Stubborn, stubborn, stubborn Luke! You like a little boy. You think this is a game? You think it don't hurt me to my heart to see you the way you is now? You think my heart ain't black with sorrow to see your soul go under?

LUKE: Stop talking about my soul. It's me, Maggie—*me!* Don't you remember *me?* Don't you care nothing about *me?* You ain't never stopped loving me. Have you, Maggie? Can't you tell me the truth?

MARGARET: Luke—we ain't young no more. It don't matter no more about us. But what about our boy? You want him to live the life you've lived? You want him to end up—old and empty-handed?

LUKE: I don't care what kind of life he lives—as long as it's *his* life —not mine, not his mama's, but his own. I ain't going to let you make him safe.

MARGARET: I can't do no more. Before God, I done my best. Your blood can't be required at my hands.

LUKE: I guess I could have told you—it weren't *my* soul we been trying to save.

(Low, syncopated singing from the church begins.)

MARGARET: Luke. You's going to die. I hope the Lord have mercy on you.

LUKE: I ain't asking for no goddam mercy. *(He turns his face to the wall.)* Go away.

MARGARET: You's going to die, Luke.

(She moves slowly from the bedroom into the kitchen. ODESSA *enters from the church, goes to* MARGARET.*)*

ODESSA: Honey—they's going to have a business meeting upstairs. You hear me? You know what that means? If you want to hold onto this church, Maggie—if you do—you better get on upstairs. (*MARGARET is silent.*) Where's David? He ought to be here when you need him.

MARGARET: I don't know.

ODESSA: I'll go and see if I can find him. You all right?

MARGARET: It looks like rain out there. Put something on.

(After a moment, ODESSA *goes.* MARGARET *walks up and down the kitchen. Her tears begin.)*

Lord, help us to stand. Help us to stand. Lord, give me strength! Give me strength!

Curtain

END OF ACT TWO

ACT III

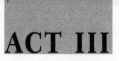

Music is heard offstage, a slow, quiet sound.

Early the following morning. A bright quiet day. Except for LUKE, the stage is empty. His room is dark. He is sleeping.

The light comes up very slowly in the church. After a moment, MRS. JACKSON enters. She is wearing a house dress and slippers. She puts her hands to her face, moaning slightly, then falls heavily before the altar.

MARGARET enters through LUKE's bedroom. She pauses a moment at the foot of LUKE's bed, then enters the kitchen, then slowly mounts to the church.

As she enters, MRS. JACKSON stirs. They stare at each other for a moment.

MRS. JACKSON is weeping.

MRS. JACKSON: Sister Margaret, you's a woman of the Lord—you say you in communion with the Lord. Why He take my baby from me? Tell me why He do it? Why He make my baby suffer so? Tell me why He do it!

MARGARET: Sister—we got to trust God—somehow. We got to bow our heads.

MRS. JACKSON: My head is bowed. My head been bowed since I been born. His daddy's head is bowed. The Lord ain't got no right to make a baby suffer so, just to make me bow my head!

MARGARET: Be careful what you say, daughter. Be careful what you say. We can't penetrate the mysteries of the Lord's will.

MRS. JACKSON (Moves away): Why I got to be careful what I say? You think the Lord going to do me something else? I ain't got to be careful what I say no more. I sit on the bench in the hospital all night long, me and my husband, and we waited and we prayed and we wept. I said, Lord, if you spare

65

my baby, I won't never take another drink, I won't do nothing, nothing to displease you, if you only give me back my baby, safe and well. He was such a nice baby and just like his daddy, he liked to laugh already. But I ain't going to have no more. Such a nice baby, I don't see why he had to get all twisted and curled up with pain and scream his little head off. And couldn't nobody help him. He hadn't never done nothing to nobody. Ain't nobody never done nothing bad enough to suffer like that baby suffered.

MARGARET: Daughter, pray with me. Come, pray with me.

MRS. JACKSON: I been trying to pray. Everytime I kneel down, I see my baby again—and—I can't pray. I can't get it out of my head, it ain't right, even if He's God, it ain't right.

MARGARET: Sister—once I lost a baby, too. I know what that emptiness feel like, I declare to my Saviour I do. That was when I come to the Lord. I wouldn't come before. Maybe the Lord is working with you now. Open your heart and listen. Maybe, out of all this sorrow, He's calling you to do His work.

MRS. JACKSON: I ain't like you, Sister Margaret. I don't want all this, all these people looking to me. I'm just a young woman, I just want my man and my home and my children.

MARGARET: But that's all I wanted. That's what I wanted! Sometimes—what we want—and what we ought to have—ain't the same. Sometime, the Lord, He take away what we want and give us what we need.

MRS. JACKSON: And do I need—that man sitting home with a busted heart? Do I need—two children in the graveyard?

MARGARET: I don't know, I ain't the Lord, I don't know what you need. You need to pray.

MRS. JACKSON: No, I'm going home to my husband. He be getting worried. He don't know where I am.

(She starts out.)

MARGARET: Sister Jackson! (MRS. JACKSON *turns*.) Why did you say you ain't going to have no more babies? You still a very young woman.

MRS. JACKSON: I'm scared to go through it again. I can't go through it again.

MARGARET: That ain't right. That ain't right. You ought to have another baby. You ought to have another baby right away. (*A pause*) Honey—is there anything you want me to do for you now, in your time of trouble?

MRS. JACKSON: No, Sister Margaret, ain't nothing you can do. (*She goes.* MARGARET *stands alone in the church.*)

MARGARET: Get on home to your husband. Go on home, to your man.
(*Downstairs,* ODESSA *enters through* LUKE's *room; pauses briefly at* LUKE's *bed, enters the kitchen. She goes to the stove, puts a match under the coffeepot.* MARGARET *stares at the altar; starts downstairs.*)

ODESSA (*Sings, under her breath*):
Some say the rose of Sharon, some say the Prince of Peace.
But I call Jesus my rock!
(MARGARET *enters.*)

ODESSA: How long you been up, Maggie?

MARGARET: I don't know. Look like I couldn't sleep.

ODESSA: You got a heavy day ahead of you.

MARGARET: I know it. David ain't come in yet?

ODESSA: No, but don't you fret. He's all right. He'll be along. It's just natural for young boys to go a little wild every now and again. Soon this'll all be over, Maggie, and when you look back on it it won't be nothing more than like you had a bad dream.

MARGARET: A bad dream!

ODESSA: They ain't going to turn you out, Maggie. They ain't crazy. They know it take a *long* time before they going to find another pastor of this church like you.

MARGARET: It won't take them so long if Sister Moore have her way. She going to be the next pastor of this church. Lord, you sure can't tell what's going on in a person's heart.

ODESSA: The Bible say the heart is deceitful above all things. And desperately wicked.

MARGARET: Who can know it? I guess whoever wrote that wasn't just thinking about the hearts of other people.

ODESSA: Maggie, you better go on in the front and lie down awhile. You got time. Sunday school ain't even started yet. I'll call you in time for you to get dressed for service.

MARGARET: I reckon I better. (*She starts out, stops.*) They talk about me letting my own house perish in sin. The Word say if you put father or mother or brother or sister or husband—or *anybody*—ahead of Him, He ain't going to have nothing to do with you on the last day.

ODESSA: Yes. The Word do say so.

MARGARET: I married that man when I weren't hardly nothing but a girl. I used to know that man, look like, just inside *out*, sometime I knowed what he was going to do before he knowed it himself. Sometime I could just look up, look up at that face, and just—*know*. Ain't no man never made me laugh the way Luke could. No, nor cry neither. I ain't never held no man until I felt his pain coming into me like little drops of acid. Odessa, I bore that man his only son. Now, you know there's still something left in my heart for that man.

ODESSA: Don't think on it, honey. Don't think on it so. Go on in front and lie down.

MARGARET: Yes. (*She starts out, stops.*) Odessa—you know what amen means?

ODESSA: Amen means—*amen.*

MARGARET: Amen means Thy will be done. Amen means So be it. I been up all morning, praying—and—I couldn't say amen. (*She goes.*)

ODESSA: Lord, have mercy. Have mercy, Lord, this morning. (*Sings, under her breath*) Some say the Rose of Sharon, some say the Prince of Peace. But I call Jesus my rock!

(*She goes to the door of* LUKE's *room.* BROTHER *and* SISTER BOXER *and* SISTER MOORE *enter the church. The two women are all in white.*)

Yes, Lord. Everytime a woman don't know if she coming or going, every*time* her heart get all swelled up with grief, there's a man sleeping somewhere close by.

(SISTER BOXER *crosses the church and comes down the stairs.*)

SISTER BOXER: Praise the Lord, Sister Odessa. You all alone this morning?

ODESSA: I didn't know you folks was upstairs. How long you been there?

SISTER BOXER: We just this minute come in.

ODESSA: You all mighty early, seems to me.

SISTER BOXER: Well, Sister Moore, she thought if we got here early we might be able to see Sister Margaret before anybody else come in.

ODESSA: Sister Margaret ain't ready to see nobody yet.

SISTER BOXER: It almost time for Sunday school.

ODESSA: Sister Boxer, you know right well that Sister Margaret don't hardly never come to Sunday school. She got to save her strength for the morning service. You know that.

SISTER BOXER: Well, Sister Moore thought—maybe *this* morning—

ODESSA: Sister Boxer—don't you think enough harm's been done with all them terrible things was said last night?

SISTER BOXER: Ain't nobody said nothing last night that wasn't the gospel truth.

ODESSA: I done heard enough truth these last couple of days to last me the rest of my life.

SISTER BOXER: The truth is a two-edged sword, Sister Odessa.

ODESSA: It ain't never going to cut you down. You ain't never going to come that close to it.

SISTER BOXER: Well—do Jesus! Soon as something happens to that sister of yours you forgets all about your salvation, don't you? You better ask the Lord to watch your tongue. The tongue is a *unruly* member.

ODESSA: It ain't as unruly as it's going to get. (*A pause*) Sister Boxer, this ain't no way for us to be talking. We used to be *friends*. We used to have right *good* times together. How come we got all this bad feeling all of a sudden? Look like it come out of nowhere, overnight.

SISTER BOXER: I ain't got no bad feeling toward *you*, Sister Odessa. (*After a moment,* SISTER BOXER *turns and mounts to the church.* ODESSA *follows.*)

SISTER MOORE: Praise the Lord, Sister Odessa. How you this Lord's day morning?

ODESSA: I'm leaning on the Lord, Sister Moore. How you feeling?

BROTHER BOXER: Praise the Lord, Sister Odessa. I'm mighty glad to hear you say that. We needs the Lord this morning. We needs to hear Him speak peace to our souls.

ODESSA: How come you folks want to see Sister Margaret so early in the morning?

SISTER BOXER: Well, we ain't really got to see Sister Margaret, not now that you're here, Sister Odessa. You is still one of the elders of this church.

SISTER MOORE: We want to do everything we got to do in front, amen. Don't want nobody saying we went around and done it in the dark.

ODESSA: You's doing it in front, all right. You's supposed to do it in front of the whole congregation this afternoon.

BROTHER BOXER: Well, the Lord's done led us to do a little different from the way we was going to do last night.

ODESSA: How's that, Brother Boxer? (*A pause*) Well, now, the way I understood it last *night*—you folks say that Margaret ain't got no right to call herself a spiritual leader. *You* folks say that Margaret done let her own household perish in sin and —you folks say—that all these things is a sign from the Lord that He ain't pleased with Margaret and you was going to put all that in front of this church and the church from Philadelphia and see what *they* thought. Ain't that right?

SISTER BOXER: We done already spoken to the members of this church. Margaret's as good as read out of this church already, ain't hardly no need for her to come to service.

SISTER MOORE: I spoke to them myself. I been up since early this morning, bless the Lord, just ringing doorbells and stirring up the people against sin.

ODESSA: You must of got up mighty early.

SISTER MOORE: When the Lord's work is to be done, I gets up out of my bed. God don't love the slothful. And, look like the more I do, the more He gives me strength to do.

BROTHER BOXER: We thought it might be easier on Sister Margaret if we done it this way. Ain't no need for folks to know all of Sister Margaret's personal business. So we ain't said nothing about Brother Luke. Folks is bound to try and put two and two together—but *we* ain't said nothing. We ain't said nothing about Brother David. We is just told the congregation that the Lord's done revealed to the elders of this church that Sister Margaret ain't been leading the life of a holy woman, especially a holy woman in *her* position, is supposed to lead. That's all. And we said we weren't sitting in *judgment* on Sister Margaret. We was leaving it up to her conscience, amen, and the Lord.

SISTER BOXER: But we did say—since we're the elders of the church and we got a responsibility to the congregation, too—that the Lord ain't pleased at Margaret sitting in the seat of authority.

SISTER MOORE: It's time for her to come down.

ODESSA: And how did folks take it when you told them all this?

BROTHER BOXER: Well, folks ain't in this church to worship Sister Margaret. They's here to worship the Lord.

ODESSA: Folks thought Margaret was good enough to be their pastor all these years, they ain't going to stop wanting her for pastor overnight.

BROTHER BOXER: She rose overnight. She can fall overnight.

SISTER BOXER: I tell you, Sister Odessa, like the song says: "You may run on a great, long time but great God Almighty going to cut you down." Yes, indeed, He going to let the truth be known one *day*. And on that day, it's just too bad *for* you. Sister Margaret done had a lot of people fooled a long time, but now, bless God forever, the truth is out.

ODESSA: What truth? What is that woman done to make you hate her so? Weren't but only yesterday you was all saying how wonderful she was, and how blessed we was to have her. And now you can't find nothing bad enough to say about her. Don't give me that stuff about her letting her household perish in sin. Ain't a one of you but ain't got a brother or a sister or somebody on the road to hell right now. I want to know what is she *done?* What is she done to you, Sister Moore?

SISTER BOXER: *I* ain't got no brothers or sisters on the road to hell. Only sister I *had* is waiting for me in glory. And every *soul* I come in contact with is saved—except of course for them people I work for. And I got no trombone-playing husband dying in my house and I ain't got no half-grown son out fornicating in the wilderness.

SISTER MOORE: Don't you come up here and act like you thought we was just acting out of spite and meanness. Your sister ain't done nothing to me; she *can't* do nothing to me because the Lord holds me in His hands. All we's trying to do is the Lord's will—you ought to be trying to do it, too. If we want to reign with him in glory, we ain't supposed to put nobody before Him. Amen! We ain't supposed to have no other love but Him.

SISTER BOXER: I looked at that man and I says to myself, How in the *world* did Sister Margaret ever get herself mixed up with a man like that?

ODESSA: Ain't no mystery how a woman gets mixed up with a man, Sister Boxer, and you sure ought to know that, even if poor Sister Moore here *don't.*

SISTER MOORE: Don't you poor-Sister-Moore *me.* That man put a demon inside your sister and that demon's walking up and down inside her still. You can see it in her eyes, they done got all sleepy with lust.

ODESSA: Sister Moore, I sure would like to know just how come *you* know so much about it.

SISTER BOXER: Sister Odessa, ain't no sense to you trying to put everybody in the wrong because Sister Margaret is falling. That ain't going to raise her back up. It's the Lord's *will* she should come down.

ODESSA: I don't understand how you can take her part against my sister. *You* ought to know how much Sister Margaret's suffered all these years by herself. *You* know it ain't no easy thing for a woman to go it alone. She done spent more'n ten years to build this up for herself and her little boy. How you going to throw her out now? What's she going to do, where's she going to go?

BROTHER BOXER: She didn't worry about Elder King when she took over this church from him.

SISTER MOORE: I think you think I hates your sister because she been married. And I ain't never been married. I ain't questioning the Lord's ways. He done kept me pure to Himself for a purpose, and that purpose is working itself out right here in this room this morning—right here in this room, this upper room. It make your sister look double-minded, I do declare it do, if she done tried, one time, to bring peace to one man, and failed, and then she jump up and think she going to bring peace to a whole lot of people.

ODESSA: Sister Margaret done give good service all those years. She ain't been acting like she was double-minded.

BROTHER BOXER: But I bet you—she is double-minded *now*.
(DAVID *enters the apartment. He is suffering from a hang-over, is still a little drunk. He goes to the sink and splashes cold water on his face. He moves with both bravado and fear and there is a kind of heart-breaking humor in his actions.*)

SISTER BOXER: Odessa, a church can't have no woman for pastor who done been married once and then decided it didn't suit her and then jump up and run off from her husband and take a seat in the pulpit and act like she ain't no woman no more. That ain't no kind of example to the young. The Word say the marriage bed is holy.

ODESSA: I can't believe—I can't *believe* you really going to do it. We been friends so long.

(DAVID *dries his face. He goes to the door of* LUKE'S *room, stands for a moment looking at his father. He turns back into the kitchen. At this moment,* MARGARET *enters, dressed in white. She and* DAVID *stare at each other.*)

SISTER BOXER: You the one I'm sorry for, Sister Odessa. You done spent your life, look like, protecting that sister of yours. And now you can't protect her no more.

ODESSA: It ain't been me protecting Sister Margaret. It been the Lord. And He ain't yet withdrawed His hand. He ain't never left none of His children alone.

(*She starts for the rear door of the church.*)

SISTER BOXER: How come you ain't never been married, Sister Odessa?

ODESSA: Suppose we just say, Sister Boxer, that I never had the time.

SISTER BOXER: It might have been better for you if you'd taken the time.

ODESSA: I ain't got no regrets. No, I ain't. I ain't claiming I'm pure, like Sister Moore here. I ain't claiming that the Lord had such special plans for me that I couldn't have nothing to do with men. Brothers and sisters, if you knew just a little bit about folks' lives, what folks go through, and the low, black places they finds their feet—you *would* have a meeting here this afternoon. Maybe I don't know the Lord like you do, but I know something else. I know how men and women can come together and change each other and make each other suffer, and make each other glad. If you putting my sister out of this church, you putting me out, too.

(*She goes out through the street door. The church dims out.*)

MARGARET: Where you been until this time in the morning, son?

DAVID: I was out visiting some people I know. And it got to be later than I realized and I stayed there overnight.

MARGARET: How come it got to be so late before you realized it?

DAVID: I don't know. We just got to talking.

MARGARET: Talking? (*She moves closer to him*) What was you talking about, son? You stink of whiskey!
(*She slaps him.* DAVID *sits at the table.*)

DAVID: That ain't going to do no good, Ma.
(*She slaps him again.* DAVID *slumps on the table, his head in his arms.*)

MARGARET: Is that what I been slaving for all these long, hard years? Is I carried slops and scrubbed floors and ate leftovers and swallowed bitterness by the gallon jugful—for this? So you could walk in here this Lord's-day morning stinking from whiskey and some no-count, dirty, black girl's sweat? Declare, I wish you'd died in my belly, too, if I been slaving all these years for this!

DAVID: Mama. Mama. Please.

MARGARET: Sit up and look at me. Is you too drunk to hold up your head? Or is you too ashamed? Lord knows you ought to be ashamed.

DAVID: Mama, I wouldn't of had this to happen this way for nothing in the world.

MARGARET: Was they holding a pistol to your head last evening? Or did they tie you down and pour the whiskey down your throat?

DAVID: No. No. Didn't nobody have no pistol. Didn't nobody have no rope. Some fellows said, Let's pick up some whiskey. And I said, Sure. And we all put in some money and I went down to the liquor store and bought it. And then we drank it.
(MARGARET *turns away.*)

MARGARET: David, I ain't so old. I know the world is wicked. I know young people have terrible temptations. Did you do it because you was afraid them boys would make fun of you?

DAVID: No.

MARGARET: Was it on account of some girl?

DAVID: No.

MARGARET: Was it—your daddy put you up to it? Was it your daddy made you think it was manly to get drunk?

DAVID: Daddy—I don't think you can blame it on Daddy, Mama.

MARGARET: Why'd you do it, David? When I done tried so hard to raise you right? Why'd you want to hurt me this way?

DAVID: I didn't want to hurt you, Mama. But this day has been coming a long time. Mama, I can't play piano in church no more.

MARGARET: Is it on account of your daddy? Is it your daddy put all this foolishness in your head?

DAVID: Daddy ain't been around for a long time, Mama. I ain't talked to him but one time since he been here.

MARGARET: And that one time—he told you all about the wonderful time he had all them years, blowing out his guts on that trombone.

DAVID: No. That ain't exactly what he said. That ain't exactly what we talked about.

MARGARET: What *did* you talk about?
(*A sound of children singing "Jesus Loves Me" comes from the church.*)

DAVID: Well—he must have been talking about you. About how he missed you, and all.

MARGARET: Sunday school done started. David, why don't you go upstairs and play for them, just this one last morning?

DAVID: Mama, I told you. I can't play piano in church no more.

MARGARET: David, why don't you feel it no more, what you felt once? Where's it gone? Where's the Holy Ghost gone?

DAVID: I don't know, Mama. It's empty. (*He indicates his chest*) It's empty here.

MARGARET: Can't you pray? Why don't you pray? If you pray, pray hard, He'll come back. The Holy Ghost will come back. He'll come down on heavenly wings, David, and (*She touches his chest*) fill that empty space, He'll start your heart to singing—singing again. He'll fill you, David, with a mighty burning fire and burn *out* (*She takes his head roughly between her palms*) all that foolishness, all them foolish dreams you carries around up there. Oh, David, David, pray that the Holy Ghost will come back, that the gift of God will come back!

DAVID: Mama, if a person don't feel it, he just don't feel it.

MARGARET: David, I'm older than you. I done been down the line. I know ain't no safety nowhere in this world if you don't stay close to God. What you think the world's got out there for you but a broken heart?
(ODESSA, *unnoticed, enters.*)

ODESSA: You better listen to her, David.

MARGARET: I remember boys like you down home, David, many years ago—fine young men, proud as horses, and I seen what happened to them. I seen them go down, David, until they was among the lowest of the low. There's boys like you down there, today, breaking rock and building roads, they ain't never going to hold up their heads up on this earth no more. There's boys like you all over this city, filling up the gin mills and standing on the corners, running down alleys, tearing themselves to pieces with knives and whiskey and dope and sin! You think I done lived this long and I don't know what's happening? Fine young men and they're lost—they don't know what's happened to their life. Fine young men, and some of them dead and some of them dead while they living. You think I want to see this happen to you? You think I want you one day lying where your daddy lies today?

ODESSA: You better listen to her David. You better listen.

MARGARET: No. He ain't going to listen. Young folks don't never listen. They just go on, headlong, and they think ain't nothing ever going to be too big for them. And, time they find out, it's too late then.

DAVID: And if I listened—what would happen? What do you think would happen if I listened? You want me to stay here, getting older, getting sicker—hating you? You think I want to hate you, Mama? You think it don't tear me to pieces to have to lie to you all the time. Yes, because I been lying to you, Mama, for a long time now! I don't want to tell no more lies. I don't want to keep on feeling so bad inside that I have to go running down them alleys you was talking about—that alley right outside this door!—to find something to help me hide—to hide—from what I'm feeling. Mama, I want to be a man. It's time you let me be a man. You got to let me go.

(A pause.)

If I stayed here—I'd end up worse than Daddy—because I wouldn't be doing what I know I got to do—I *got* to do! I've seen your life—and now I see Daddy—and I love you, I love you both!—but I've got my work to do, something's happening in the world out there, I got to go! I know you think I don't know what's happening, but I'm beginning to see—something. Every time I play, every time I listen, I see Daddy's face and yours, and so many faces—who's going to speak for all that, Mama? Who's going to speak for all of us? I can't stay home. Maybe I can say something—one day

—maybe I can say something in music that's never been said before. Mama—*you* knew this day was coming.

MARGARET: I reckon I thought I was Joshua and could make the sun stand still.

DAVID: Mama, I'm leaving this house tonight. I'm going on the road with some other guys. I got a lot of things to do today and I ain't going to be hanging around the house. I'll see you before I go.

(*He starts for the door.*)

MARGARET: David—?

DAVID: Yes, Mama?

MARGARET: Don't you want to eat something?

DAVID: No, Mama. I ain't hungry now.

(*He goes.*)

MARGARET: Well. There he go. Who'd ever want to love a man and raise a child! Odessa—you think I'm a hard woman?

ODESSA: No. I don't think you a hard woman. But I think you's in a hard place.

MARGARET: I done something, somewhere, wrong.

ODESSA: Remember this morning. You got a awful thing ahead of you this morning. You got to go upstairs and win them folks back to you this morning.

MARGARET: My man is in there, dying, and my baby's in the world— how'm I going to preach, Odessa? How'm I going to preach when I can't even pray?

ODESSA: You got to face them. You got to think. You got to pray.

MARGARET: Sister, I can't. I can't. I can't.

ODESSA: Maggie. It was you had the vision. It weren't me. You got to think back to the vision. If the vision was for anything, it was for just this day.

MARGARET: The vision. Ah, it weren't yesterday, that vision. I was in a cold, dark place and I thought it was the grave. And I listened to hear my little baby cry and didn't no cry come. I heard a voice say, Maggie. Maggie. You got to find you a hiding place. I wanted Luke. (*She begins to weep.*) Oh, sister, I don't remember no vision. I just remember that it was dark and I was scared and my baby was dead and I wanted Luke, I wanted Luke, I wanted Luke!

ODESSA: Oh, honey. Oh, my honey. What we going to do with you this morning? (MARGARET *cannot stop weeping.*) Come on, honey, come on. You got them folks to face.

MARGARET: All these years I prayed as hard as I knowed how. I tried to put my treasure in heaven where couldn't nothing get at it and take it away from me and leave me alone. I asked the Lord to hold my hand. I didn't expect that none of this would ever rise to hurt me no more. And all these years it just been waiting for me, waiting for me to turn a corner. And there it stand, my whole life, just like I hadn't never gone nowhere. It's a awful thing to think about, the way love never dies!

ODESSA: You's got to pull yourself together and think how you can *win*. You always been the winner. Ain't no time to be a woman *now*. You can't let them throw you out of this church. What we going to do then? I'm getting old, I can't help you. And you ain't young no more, neither.

MARGARET: Maybe we could go—someplace else.

ODESSA: We ain't got no money to go no place. We ain't paid the rent for this month. We ain't even finished paying for this Frigidaire.

MARGARET: I remember in the old days whenever Luke wanted to spend some money on foolishness, that is exactly what I would have to say to him: "Man, ain't you got good sense? Do you know we ain't even paid the rent for this month?"

ODESSA: Margaret. You got to think.

MARGARET: Odessa, you remember when we was little there was a old blind woman lived down the road from us. She used to live in this house all by herself and you used to take me by the hand when we walked past her house because I was scared of her. I can see her, just as plain somehow, sitting on the porch, rocking in that chair, just looking out over them roads like she could see something. And she used to hear us coming, I guess, and she'd shout out, "How you this Lord's-day morning?" Don't care what day it was, or what time of day it was, it was always the Lord's-day morning for her. Daddy used to joke about her, he used to say, "Ain't no man in that house. It's a mighty sad house." I reckon this going to be a mighty sad house before long.

ODESSA: Margaret. You got to think.

MARGARET: I'm thinking. I'm thinking. I'm thinking how I throwed away my life.

ODESSA: You can't think about it like that. You got to remember— you gave your life to the Lord.

MARGARET: I'm thinking now—maybe Luke needed it more. Maybe David could of used it better. I know. I got to go upstairs and face them people. Ain't nothing else left for me to do. I'd like to talk to Luke.

ODESSA: I'll go on up there.

MARGARET: The only thing my mother should have told me is that being a woman ain't nothing but one long fight with men. And even the Lord, look like, ain't nothing but the most impossible kind of man there is. Go on upstairs, sister. Be there—when I get there.

(After a moment, ODESSA goes. Again, we hear the sound of singing: "God be with you till we meet again."

MARGARET *walks into* LUKE's *bedroom, stands there a moment, watching him.*

82

BROTHER BOXER *enters the kitchen, goes to the Frigidaire, pours himself a Kool-aid.*)

MARGARET (*Turns*): What are you doing down here, Brother Boxer? Why ain't you upstairs in the service?

BROTHER BOXER: Why ain't *you* upstairs in the service, Sister Margaret? We's waiting for you upstairs.

MARGARET: I'm coming upstairs! Can't you go on back up there now and ask them folks to be—a little quiet? He's sick, Brother Boxer. He's sick!

BROTHER BOXER: You just finding that out? He *been* sick, Sister Margaret. How come it ain't never upset you until now? And how you expect me to go upstairs and ask them folks to be quiet when you been telling us all these years to praise the Lord with fervor? Listen! They got fervor. Where's all your fervor done gone to, Sister Margaret?

MARGARET: Brother Boxer, even if you don't want me for your pastor no more, please remember I'm a woman. Don't talk to me this way.

BROTHER BOXER: A woman? Is *that* where all your fervor done gone to? You trying to get back into that man's arms, Sister Margaret? What you want him to do for you—you want him to take off that long white robe?

MARGARET: Be careful, Brother Boxer. It ain't over yet. It ain't over yet.

BROTHER BOXER: Oh, yes it is, Sister Margaret. It's over. You just don't know it's over. Come on upstairs. Maybe you can make those folks keep quiet.
(*The music has stopped.*)
They's quiet now. They's waiting for you.

MARGARET: You hate me. How long have you hated me? What have I ever done to make you hate me?

BROTHER BOXER: All these years you been talking about how the Lord done called you. Well, you sure come running but I ain't so sure you was called. I seen you in there, staring at that man. You ain't no better than the rest of them. You done sweated and cried in the nighttime, too, and you'd like to be doing it again. You had me fooled with that long white robe but you ain't no better. You ain't as good. You been sashaying around here acting like weren't nobody good enough to touch the hem of your garment. You was always so pure, Sister Margaret, you made the rest of us feel like dirt.

MARGARET: I was trying to please the Lord.

BROTHER BOXER: And you reckon you did? Declare, I never thought I'd see you so quiet. All these years I been running errands for you, saying, Praise the Lord, Sister Margaret. That's *right*, Sister Margaret! Amen, Sister Margaret! I didn't know if you even knew what a man was. I never thought I'd live long enough to find out that Sister Margaret weren't nothing but a woman who run off from her husband and then started ruling other people's lives because she didn't have no man to control her. I sure hope you make it into heaven, girl. You's too late to catch any other train.

MARGARET: It's not over yet. It's not over.

BROTHER BOXER: You coming upstairs?

MARGARET: I'm coming.

BROTHER BOXER: Well. We be waiting.

(*He goes.* MARGARET *stands alone in the kitchen. As* BROTHER BOXER *enters, the lights in the church go up. The church is packed. Far in the back* SISTER ODESSA *sits.* SISTER MOORE *is in the pulpit, and baritone soloist is singing.*)

BARITONE:

Soon I'll be done with the troubles of the world,
Troubles of the world, troubles of the world,

Soon I'll be done with the troubles of the world,
Going home to live with my Lord.

Soon I'll be done with the troubles of the world,
Troubles of the world, troubles of the world,
Soon I'll be done with the troubles of the world,
Going home to live with my Lord.

Soon I'll be done with the troubles of the world,
Troubles of the world, troubles of the world,
Soon I'll be done with the troubles of the world,
Going home to live with my Lord.

SISTER MOORE (*Reads*): For if after they have escaped the pollution of the world through the knowledge of the Lord and Saviour Jesus Christ they are again entangled therein and overcome, the latter end is worse with them than the beginning.

ALL: Amen!

SISTER MOORE (*Reads*): For it had been better for them not to have known the way of righteousness than after they had known it to turn away from the holy commandment delivered unto them. Amen! Sister Boxer, would you read the last verse for us? Bless our God!

SISTER BOXER (*Reads*): But it is happened unto them according to the true proverb, the dog is turned to his own vomit again and the sow that was washed to her wallowing in the mire. (*The church dims out.* MARGARET *walks into the bedroom.*)

MARGARET: Luke?

LUKE: Maggie. Where's my son?

MARGARET: He's gone, Luke. I couldn't hold him. He's gone off into the world.

LUKE: He's gone?

MARGARET: He's gone.

LUKE: He's gone into the world. He's into the world!

MARGARET: Luke, you won't never see your son no more.

LUKE: But I seen him one last time. He's in the world, he's living.

MARGARET: He's gone. Away from you and away from me.

LUKE: He's living. He's living. Is you got to see your God to know he's living.

MARGARET: Everything—is dark this morning.

LUKE: You all in white. Like you was the day we got married. You mighty pretty.

MARGARET: It were a sunny day. Like today.

LUKE: Yeah. They used to say, "Happy is the bride the sun shines on."

MARGARET: Yes. That's what they used to say.

LUKE: Was you happy that day, Maggie?

MARGARET: Yes.

LUKE: I loved you, Maggie.

MARGARET: I know you did.

LUKE: I love you still.

MARGARET: I know you do.

(They embrace and singing is heard from the darkened church: "The Old Ship of Zion.")

Maybe it's not possible to stop loving anybody you ever really loved. I never stopped loving you, Luke. I tried. But I never stopped loving you.

LUKE: I'm glad you's come back to me, Maggie. When your arms was around me I was always safe and happy.

MARGARET: Oh, Luke! If we could only start again!

(His mouthpiece falls from his hand to the floor.)

Luke?

(*He does not answer.*)

My baby. You done joined hands with the darkness.

(*She rises, moving to the foot of the bed, her eyes on* LUKE. *She sees the mouthpiece, picks it up, looks at it.*)

My Lord! If I could only start again! If I could only start again!

(*The light comes up in the church. All, except* ODESSA, *are singing, "I'm Gonna Sit at the Welcome Table," clapping, etc.* SISTER MOORE *leads the service from the pulpit. Still holding* LUKE's *mouthpiece clenched against her breast,* MARGARET *mounts into the church. As she enters, the music dies.*)

MARGARET: Praise the Lord!

SISTER MOORE: You be careful, Sister Margaret. Be careful what you say. You been uncovered.

MARGARET: I come up here to put you children on your knees! Don't you know the Lord is displeased with every one of you? Have every one of you forgot your salvation? Don't **you** know that it is *forbidden*—amen!—to talk against the Lord's anointed? Ain't a soul under the sound of my voice—bless God!—who has the right to sit in judgment on my life! Sister Margaret, this woman you see before you, has given her life to the Lord—and you say the Lord is displeased with me because ain't a one of you willing to endure what I've endured. Ain't a one of you willing to go—the road I've walked. This way of holiness ain't no joke. You can't love the Lord and flirt with the Devil. The Word of God is right and the Word of God is plain—and you can't love God unless you's willing to give up everything for Him. Everything.

I want you folks to pray. I want every one of you to go down on your knees. We going to have a tarry service here tonight. Oh, yes! David, you play something on that piano—

(She stops, stares at the piano, where one of the saints from Philadelphia is sitting.)

David—David—

(She looks down at her fist.)

Oh, my God.

SISTER BOXER: Look at her! *Look* at her! The gift of God has left her!

MARGARET: Children. I'm just now finding out what it means to love the Lord. It ain't all in the singing and the shouting. It ain't all in the reading of the Bible. *(She unclenches her fist a little.)* It ain't even—it ain't even—in running all over everybody trying to get to heaven. To love the Lord is to love all His children—all of them, everyone!—and suffer with them and rejoice with them and never count the cost!

(Silence. She turns and leaves the pulpit.)

SISTER MOORE: Bless our God! He give us the victory! I'm gonna feast on milk and honey.

(She is joined by the entire congregation in this final song of jubilation.

MARGARET *comes down the stairs. She stands in the kitchen.* ODESSA *comes downstairs. Without a word to* MARGARET, *she goes through* LUKE's *room, taking off her robe as she goes. The lights dim down in the church, dim up on* MARGARET, *as* MARGARET *starts toward the bedroom, and falls beside* LUKE's *bed.*

The scrim comes down. One or two people pass in the street.)

Curtain

END OF ACT THREE

ALSO BY JAMES BALDWIN

"One of the few genuinely indispensable American writers."
—*Saturday Review*

BLUES FOR MISTER CHARLIE

In a small southern town, a white man murders a black man, then throws his body in the weeds. With this act of violence—which is loosely based on the notorious 1955 killing of Emmett Till—James Baldwin launches an unsparing and at times agonizing probe of the wounds of race.

Drama/Literature/0-679-76178-0

NOBODY KNOWS MY NAME

This is a collection of illuminating, deeply felt essays on topics ranging from race relations in the United States to the role of the writer in society, with personal accounts of such writers as Richard Wright and Norman Mailer.

Literature/African American Studies/0-679-74473-8

THE FIRE NEXT TIME

At once a powerful evocation of his early life in Harlem and a disturbing examination of the consequences of racial injustice—to both the individual and the body politic—*The Fire Next Time*, which galvanized the nation in the early days of the civil rights movement, stands as one of the essential works of our literature.

Literature/African American Studies/0-679-74472-X

ALSO AVAILABLE:

Another Country, 0-679-74471-1
Going to Meet the Man, 0-679-76179-9

Available at your local bookstore, or call toll-free to order:
1-800-793-2665 (credit cards only).